the
artist's
silkscreen
manual

the artist's silkscreen manual

andrew b. gardner

grosset & dunlap, publishers, new york, a filmways company

Copyright © 1976 by Andrew B. Gardner
All rights reserved
Published simultaneously in Canada
Library of Congress catalog card number:
  73-22737
ISBN: 0-448-11593-X (paperback edition)
ISBN: 0-448-13322-9 (library edition)
1981 Printing
Printed in the United States of America

contents

preface

The Silkscreen is as modern as plastics. It is everywhere, yet it goes practically unnoticed. It is adaptable and imitative. And it is regarded by some as a process and a form of a lower order than other processes and forms of printmaking. Like plastics, the silkscreen lacks a prestige attached to other processes, and some artists tend to turn up their noses and ignore its particular properties in favor of more traditional materials and forms.

It is true that the silkscreen, unlike other printing or printmaking processes, does not have an intrinsic appearance. It is not confined to printing on paper. Not only can it be applied to a great many materials, but it can also be used to create a wide range of appearances, from dead flat to high gloss, from opaque to translucent to transparent. It can be printed so thin as to have no discernible thickness; it can be printed so thick and textured as to appear to be another material laminated to the printed surface.

For an idea of what can be done with silkscreen, look more closely at the printed items all around you. Many billboards are silkscreened. Practically all decals. All commercial ceramic decorations. Many greeting cards, posters, bumper stickers, and textiles—from sweat shirts and pennants to the most intricate and exclusive prints. Practically all printing on illuminated plastic signs, displays, vending machines. Plastic and glass bottles. Highway signs. And, of course, there is the continually expanding use in fine arts—such as printmaking, painting and sculpture.

Perhaps it is this very versatility that causes some people to hold the silkscreen in disdain as a lesser form of printing or printmaking. For the silkscreen is not easily identifiable or recognizable for what it is, and like many things in American society, that which defies easy labeling tends to be viewed with suspicion.

This book is intended to help people to come to terms with the entire range of the silkscreen, to see that its technical and artistic virtuosity and versatility do not imply complexity or great cost. For of all the printing and printmaking processes, it is the easiest and cheapest; and it is the most expedient method of generating multiple images in limited quantities. Unlike other printing processes, the tools, techniques, and materials of the silkscreen artist are exactly the same as those of the commercial printer.

This book is therefore primarily a how-to-do-it book. It covers the full range of techniques of the silkscreen artist and a wide range of materials for silkscreening on paper and similar materials. It covers the techniques and materials for making decals, beading and flocking, etching and lithography plates, glass etching, and printing on and forming plastic. It touches on ceramic and textile techniques and materials. It is, of course, not meant to be all things to all people. Those who are interested in pursuing more specialized techniques and applications will, however, have no difficulty in generalizing from the discussions here to other areas that use more costly, more complicated materials.

The intent is thus to provide a great deal of information and to make it available cheaply to those who are beginning in silkscreen. No glowing color reproductions are included, and no aesthetic principles are laid down as to what to try to achieve in the final print.

The beginning student will wish to gain a sense of accomplishment and even a beginner's mastery before coming to the end of his study. However, the material is not presented in textbook style, with exercises to demonstrate mastery of a single technique before progressing to another. Rather, it is presented in the manner of a compendium arranged around the elements of the art. An artist spends much of his time on the design, on finding the images he wants to achieve, and considering the techniques he will use to achieve them. Decisions about the graphic quality of the final print will go far to determine which techniques to use. In silkscreen printing, many such decisions have to be made. For example, a desire to have a hard-edged image in the final print will influence the choice of screen, ink, stencil, and squeegee. Questions of expediency and cost will also arise when two different techniques may be used to achieve the same effect. The material presented here is integrated to allow consideration of all these factors, and the beginner should therefore read through the entire book before using the appropriate sections to master separate elements of the process. The book permits use when an instructor is not around to guide you.

It is hoped that **The Artist's Silkscreen Manual** will allow you to obtain beginning mastery of silkscreen techniques. If you follow the guides contained here, you may not become a great artist—or, at least, not immediately—but you will not be confronted with the disasters that arise from working alone.

1.
equipment, materials,

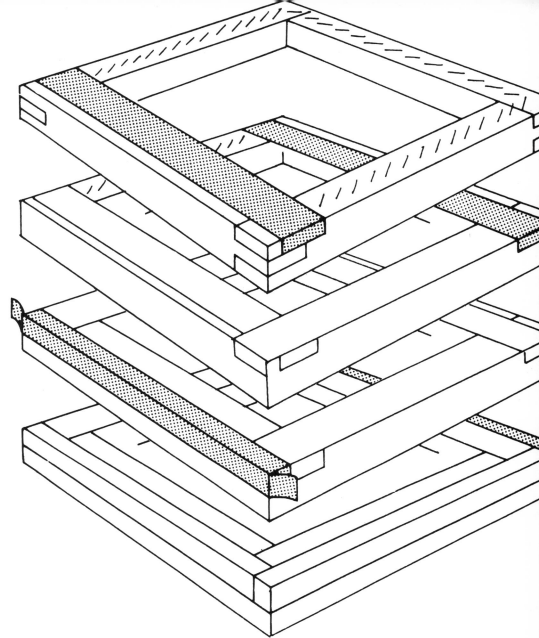

and supplies

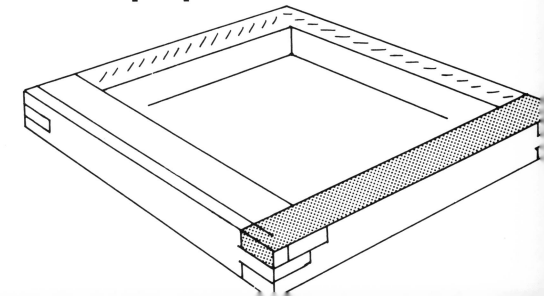

Whatever the application, use, or function, silkscreen printing requires certain basic equipment, materials, and supplies. The basic equipment consists of a frame covered with a fine, tightly stretched fabric—that is, a screen—a surface to print on, to which the screen is hinged, ink, and a squeegee to apply the ink.

THE SCREEN: WHEN TO BUILD AND WHEN TO BUY

Traditionally, artists have built their own screens as they needed them, and built them with the idea that the screens are permanent pieces of equipment. Though there will be many times when, of necessity, this will still be the case, the great growth of commercial silkscreen printing and changes in artists' attitudes toward using the services of specialists have had an impact.

Now it is possible in most large cities to find a screen processor or supplier who will provide screens, made to order, within twenty-four to forty-eight hours. A screen 30" x 40", stretched with a good quality fabric—generally silk or dacron in a 12xx mesh—and constructed of good quality straight pine, may cost as little as $14 and may be ordered over the phone.

Since obtaining the necessary materials may require a trip to a lumber yard, a trip to a hardware store, and a final expedition to the processor for the fabric, it is clear that making the screen yourself is not exactly expedient. And since making use of these materials assumes possession of certain tools and skills and the time in which to use them, it is clearer still that building screens may not even be economical. Finally, the resulting homemade screen will probably not be of better quality than the commercially made screen. Consequently, although am a firm believer in doing things myself, I rely more and more on the services of the processor and supplier. Time is as valuable to the artist as it is to the commercial printer.

By "commercially made screen" I mean those screens that are made to order by screen processors and suppliers, **not** the screen printing units sold through art and hobby stores, which are generally greatly overpriced and made of poor materials and with inferior craftsmanship.

Still, I build and restretch screens and keep at hand the supplies and materials needed to do so. Generally, these are small screens or screens needed in an emergency. And when I'm short on money and long on time, I make my own. My homemade screens rarely exceed 24" x 30", although I have stretched screens as large as 2' x 10'.

THE SILKSCREEN FRAME

The silkscreen frame is most often made of clear, straight pine, although spruce, cedar, birch, redwood, and even mahogany, may be used. In industrial printing, where extremely strong and precise screens are needed, aluminum, magnesium, and stainless steel frames are used.

Although clear, knot-free wood is preferred, it is of greater importance that the wood be straight and dry. If the wood is damp, wet, or uncured, it may warp, even if it was straight when purchased.

With clear wood the absence of knots makes the stapling of the fabric to the frame easier. Number two construction grade pine 2" x 2" or 2" x 4" can be good, but it should be inspected carefully before purchasing. When available, spruce will generally be straighter and cleaner than the same grade of pine.

The dimensions of the wood depend on the size of the frame. Screen processors usually use 2" x 2" lumber, and some provide lumber with a slot for stretching with a cord.

For a screen under 18" square, 1" x 2" or 1" x 3" lumber can be used, as illustrated in Figure 1.1. If the screen is larger, wood this size will bend or flex too much under the tension of the stretched fabric, and may warp.

For screens from 18" square to 48" square, it is best to use 2" x 2" lumber.

1.1 Construction of small screen with 1" x 2" or 1" x 3" lumber, showing how squeegee is supported.

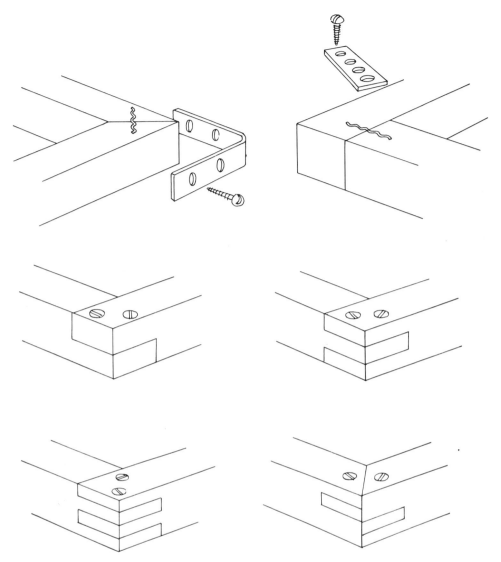

1.2 Various joints used for screen frames. From top left: miter, butt, lap, simple tongue-and-groove, double tongue-and-groove, miter tongue-and-groove.

For larger screens, it is best to use 2″ x 3″ or 2″ x 4″ lumber.

There are many ways to join the frame members. Easiest are the butt and miter joints, but neither of these is rigid without additional support, such as corrugated fasteners or corner braces (Figure 1.2). The lap joint and the tongue-and-groove joint are better, and are most commonly used by the processor, but the artist may not have the tools needed to make them.

However the frame is constructed, it should be rigid, square, and absolutely flat. Any flimsiness, twist, or out-of-square will probably result in a warped screen—a great nuisance during printing or stencil adhesion.

SCREEN FABRICS

The traditional material for the screen is silk, though the great growth of specialized and precision work has necessitated the development of other fabrics that have properties different from silk or are superior to it in various ways. Nylon, dacron, polyester, stainless steel, and phosphor bronze are all in use today.

Silk fabric is made of a fine, and fairly uniform, thread composed of many twisted fibers (Figure 1.3). It is available in three weights and a wide variety of meshes. The most common weight is double weight, called xx, and the most common mesh is 12, which is about 120 threads per inch.

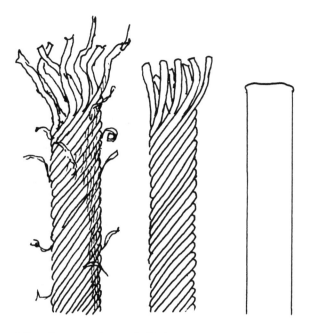

1.3   A comparison of silk (left), dacron, and nylon (exaggerated).

Silk's strength, durability, and resistance to a wide range of solvents and inks have made it the fabric of choice of many silk-screen amateurs and artists. However, its dimensional stability is poor; it relaxes under prolonged tension and is greatly affected by changes in temperature and humidity.

Since the silk threads are made of many twisted fibers, the material is extremely absorbent. This makes stencil adhesion excellent for all kinds of stencil processes, but it also causes blurring of printed edges and a loading up of ink in the screen. Often enough, in fine halftone work this causes significant breakdown of the image and seriously affects the quality of the printed image.

Although silk is resistant to many solvents and cleaners, it is not resistant to the straight chlorine bleach that is needed to remove stencils in several direct photographic processes. In fact, any strong bleach causes silk to decompose.

Recent developments are rapidly making silk an obsolete fabric. Its price has doubled in recent years, and dacron is now half as expensive. Since commercially the need is for fabrics that can be used with photo stencils, many smaller suppliers have stopped stocking silk altogether.

For many years nylon was a popular alternative to silk. Early nylon was affected by certain solvents and was particularly unstable under tension and with changes in atmospheric conditions. New nylons are vastly improved, being resistant to any solvent used and quite stable. For photographic work they are the fabrics most used. But since nylons are monofilaments, they are in most cases unsuitable for use with solvent-adhering stencils.

A more popular fabric today is dacron. It has a multifilament thread and is resistant to all solvents. Since it is extremely stable, it is also a good choice when close registration is required.

For extremely precise and finely detailed industrial work, such as printed electrical circuits, polyester fabrics are best. They are superior to silk, dacron, and nylon in dimensional stability. And because they have great durability, they are chosen for use in very long printing runs or when abrasive materials are used in printing.

Stainless steel and phosphor bronze screens provide the ultimate in durability and dimensional stability. Their cost prohibits their use by most artists, and even commercially they are not generally used except for high-precision printing.

Although, commercially, silk is falling into disuse, the codes that describe silk meshes are still used when describing other fabrics, whatever the kind, stencil technique, ink, or printing situation. The problem then confronting the artist is to translate a recommended silk mesh into an equivalent monofilament. Generally, the monofilaments (such as nylon) have a finer thread than multifilaments (such as silk or dacron). The result is that the percentage of open screen (the size of the opening between the threads) will not be the same for 16xx (155 mesh) silk and 155 mesh nylon. Since for much screen work the finest mesh possible is desired, the size of the space between threads becomes more significant than the mesh count.

There is considerable variation in all types of fabrics and meshes; therefore creative decision-making must take place at times. For instance, you may discover that 16xx silk varies in mesh from 152 to

157 threads per inch, that the space between threads varies from .0032 to .0038 inch, and that the percentage of open screen varies from 29 to 30 percent. If you decide that the opening between the threads is the most important criterion for comparison, you might find that nylons with the same opening range in mesh from 166 to 205 threads per inch and that the percentage of open screen ranges from 44 to 34 percent. As a rule, you may safely increase the mesh count of a monofilament by 25 to 33 percent over the recommended mesh for a silk or multifilament.

STRETCHING THE FABRIC

All fabrics, except steel and bronze, can be stretched by hand without the use of any tensioning device. If the screen fabric is silk, one must remember that it is particularly susceptible to humidity; it stretches on humid days and shrinks on dry days. Whenever possible, stretch silk on damp days; otherwise the screen may become slack enough to cause printing problems.

Stretching pliers are available, but canvas pliers should not be used with silk unless the jaws have been padded to prevent tearing the fabric. Other fairly inexpensive tensioning devices (Figure 1.4) are slowly disappearing from the market.

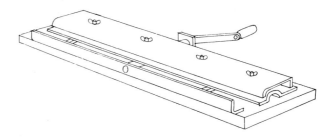

1.4   A simple screen tensioning device.

The most common method of stretching the fabric is the thumb-and-forefinger grip and knuckle-pry technique (Figure 1.5).

There are several ways to adhere the screen to the frame. All serve the purpose of achieving a tight, uniform, square, flat screen.

One popular method of stretching and adhering the fabric, the slot-and-cord method, requires that the frame be made of specially slotted lumber. A special cord is forced over the silk into the slot, pulling and tightening the fabric as it attaches it to the frame. The procedure is as follows:

1.   Cut the fabric slightly larger than the frame.

2.   Soak the fabric in water and stretch

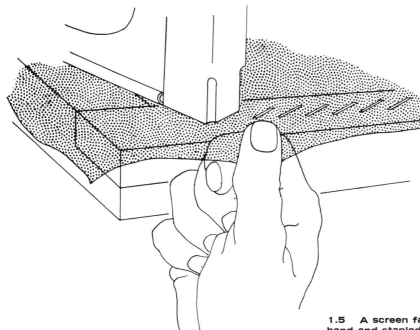

1.5   A screen fabric being tensioned with one hand and stapled to frame with the other.

EQUIPMENT, MATERIALS, AND SUPPLIES   **13**

it over the frame. The wet fabric clings to the frame and stays in position during the next step.

3.   Starting at one corner, and using a hammer, set the cord into the slot over the fabric. To ensure uniform and maximum tension with the final stretching, after the first two sides are set, apply a slight tension to the fabric while hammering in the cord on the last two sides.

4.   Starting at one end and using one of

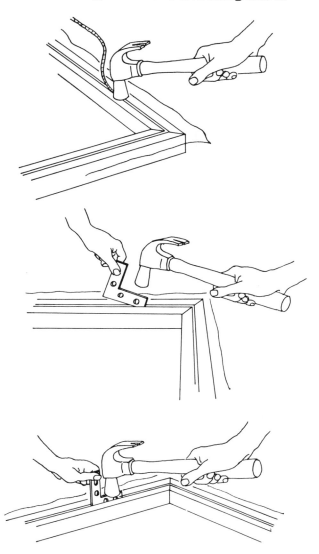

1.6   The cord-and-slot method of tensioning and attaching screen fabric to frame. Top: With fabric held flat across screen, cord is started into slot with a hammer. Middle: Cord being driven about halfway down with hammer and angle iron. Bottom: Final tensioning by driving cord to bottom of slot.

the special tools or a 3-inch flat angle iron, force the cord halfway into the slot (Figure 1.6). Make certain that the fabric does not bunch up or pucker under the cord. Do this on all four sides.

5.   Starting at one end, drive the cord all the way down. The last two sides do the final tensioning; all remaining slack must be taken up and the screen must be uniformly and tightly stretched. Be careful not to tear the fabric when going around corners.

6.   Once the screen is stretched, apply a coat of shellac along the slot to prevent the silk from slipping.

This method is probably the easiest and the fastest for stretching screens without elaborate tensioning devices. The lumber and cord are readily available from screen suppliers, but in a pinch venetian-blind cord can be used.

When using staples to attach the fabric to the screen, the thumb-and-forefinger grip and knuckle-pry technique are enough to tension the silk, since no tools or special skills are required. Basically, the fabric is pulled tight with one hand while it is stapled with the other. This may be done in several different patterns, all equally effective (Figure 1.7).

In all methods, the fabric should be an inch or so larger on all sides than the outside dimension of the frame to provide for a good grip. It is essential to pull the fabric as tight as possible in the prescribed direction: it is impossible to pull it too tight by hand. If you are using pliers, care should be taken to prevent tearing the fabric. Since the area of fabric grasped either by the hand or by pliers is small, the hand or the pliers must be moved and the fabric retensioned approximately every three staples.

The staples may be driven in several different arrangements (Figure 1.8). Generally, a single course of angled staples suffices, whereas with parallel staples a second course is needed to fill in the spaces. The advantage of the parallel courses is that additional tension can be applied as the staples are driven. Most light staple guns are suitable for use, but none drives the heads of the staples deep enough into the frame to exert uniform pressure on the fabric along the full length of the staple head. To prevent tearing of the fabric at the legs of the staples, the staples must be hammered into the frame as you go

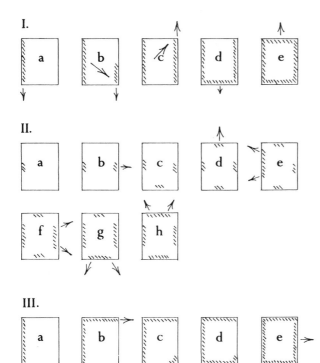

1.7 Three methods of stapling screen fabric to frame. Arrows indicate direction in which fabric is tensioned while stapling.

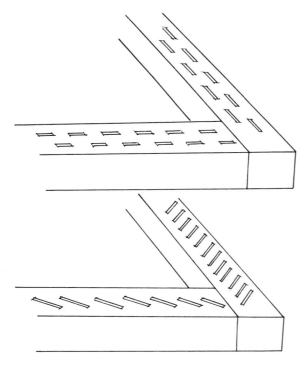

1.8 Two methods of positioning staples when stretching screen fabric.

along. This will also produce a smoother surface when you are printing in close contact.

To facilitate removal of old fabric and staples, some people staple thin strips of cardboard to the frame before stretching the fabric, and the staples holding the fabric then pass through the cardboard. To remove the fabric, one has only to pull up the strips of cardboard. Another advantage here is that the staples tend to go down flush during tensioning and stapling, eliminating the need for hammering the staples in.

When tensioning devices are available, it is possible to glue the fabric to the frame. At least two devices are needed, one on either side of the frame. A good quality cement, such as Ply-Bond, is then used.

MASKING THE SCREEN

Most printing situations require a mask between the fabric and the frame, both inside and out, to prevent the ink from flowing underneath the frame onto the printing surface. Masking also makes clean-up easier, which is especially important with screens built for long use with many changes of ink and stencils. Masking also prevents tears at the staples from developing into runs.

For such a mask a good quality kraft gummed tape, 3 inches wide, is commonly used. As it dries, it shrinks, and this tends to distribute the tension of the fabric evenly. (Solvent-proof, pressure-sensitive tapes, both in paper and cloth, are also available.)

The dimensions of the mask should suit your purpose. A large mask 3 or 4 inches wide can serve as an ink reservoir during printing and aid in applying liquid block-outs or resists, but it also greatly reduces the printing area of the screen. When the mask is to serve as a reservoir and is being applied permanently, a width of 3 to 4 inches at the narrow ends and 1 to 2 inches along the sides should be provided.

Masking is applied to the outside of the screen first, starting with the inside edge, and each succeeding strip of tape overlaps the previous one. To moisten the tape, put

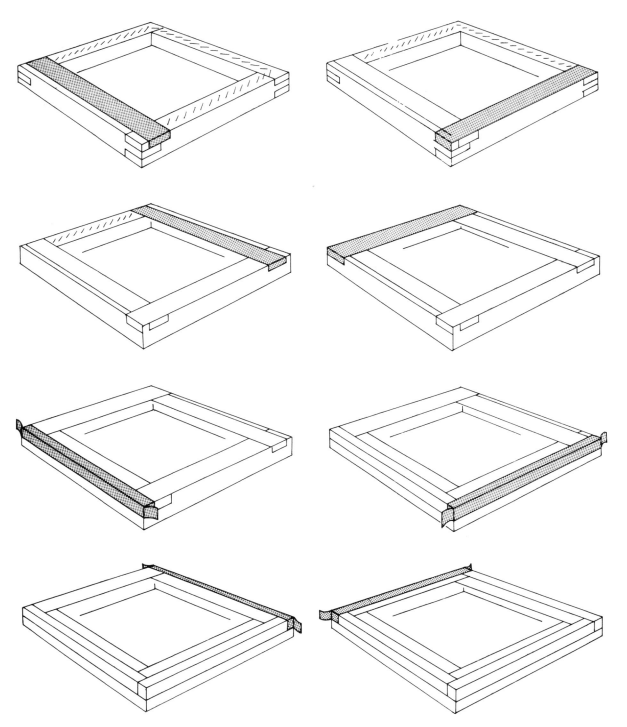

1.9   Procedure for masking screen. Shaded area represents strip of tape that is being applied.

a soaking wet sponge in a shallow dish with some water in it. Pass the tape **once** over the sponge. (If the tape is not wet after one pass, the sponge is not wet enough. Don't try wetting it again, because some of the glue will wash away and it won't adhere properly.) Lay the wet tape into position quickly and briskly rub it down, paying particular attention to the exposed edge (Figure 1.9).

Follow the same procedure for the inside of the screen, but beginning the mask about ⅛ inch nearer the frame. This minimizes the thickness of the tape at the edges and makes it easier to achieve sharply printed edges when you are printing close to the mask (Figure 1.10).

After taping is completed, inside and out, the inside corners should be masked as shown in Figure 1.11.

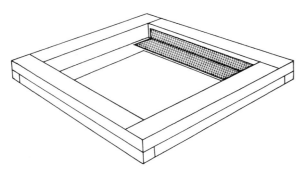

1.10 The position of the inside tape mask (shaded area) shown in relation to the outside tape mask.

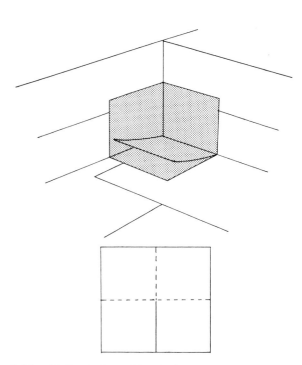

1.11 Method of masking inside corner. A 2- or 3-inch piece of tape is folded (dotted line) and cut (solid line) as shown.

SEALING THE MASK

For a permanent mask, two or three coats of orange shellac are applied to the tape and frame after the tape is dry. The shellac prevents the paper from absorbing ink and makes for easier and more complete cleanup after printing.

If masking tape is used as a mask, shellac it heavily to prevent the solvents in the ink from dissolving the cement. Unfortunately, shellac does not adhere well to masking tape, flaking off with use.

If a screen masked with kraft tape is to be used with water-soluble stencils or block-outs, it is doubly important to seal it well with shellac to prevent the water from dissolving the glue on the tape as well.

One can use shellac or lacquer. I find that shellac is not as soluble in lacquer thinner as is lacquer. I also prefer a 4- or 5-pound cut of orange shellac, as it is heavier and resistant to cracking, solvents, and abrasion. White shellac usually comes only in 3-pound cuts (3 pounds of shellac dissolved in one gallon of alcohol) and has been refined or bleached, reducing its strength.

When applying the shellac, extend it about ⅛ inch into the open fabric to ensure that the exposed edge of the tape is properly sealed (Figure 1.12).

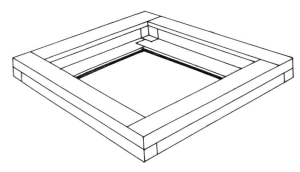

1.12 Shaded area shows that shellac extends into the fabric about ⅛ inch.

TO MASK OR NOT TO MASK

If you plan to use nearly the full size of the screen in printing, a mask of some kind is desirable. If, however, you plan to use oversized screens, a mask is not so important. Similarly, if you plan to use lacquer stencils, a sealer is not necessary. If you decide not to mask the screen, paint a couple of coats of shellac over the staples to prevent the silk from tearing.

SIZING REMOVAL

Silk has a sizing applied to it during manufacture to give it body. It is not essential to remove this sizing before using the silk. Occasionally, however, it is wise to wash a silkscreen in hot water to shrink it and to distribute tension more evenly. If you must clean or shrink a screen, use water as hot as you can stand it and a mild kitchen cleanser or laundry soap. Scrub with a rag, not a brush, for a brush will abrade the threads and raise too much nap. Rinse the screen well to remove all traces of soap or cleanser.

PRINTING SURFACE

The prepared screen must be securely hinged to a printing surface to permit accurate and repeated registration during printing. The surface may be a separate unit or a table top. In either case, the surface must be smooth, clean, and impervious to any solvents used in clean-up. Formica surfaces are best since they are absolutely flat, free from texture, and completely impervious to solvents. Tempered Masonite is good because it is exceedingly smooth and resistant to solvents. Enameled Masonite is an excellent compromise between these two, since the surface is smooth and impervious and it is considerably cheaper than Formica. For rigidity these materials should be cemented to a piece of ⅜-inch plywood or Nova-Ply with a good quality contact cement. (Nails or screws can distort the surface.)

A table top, if used, must also be smooth and even, free of all bumps and depressions, since even a small bump may cause a hole to be worn in the screen in a very short time. The finish should be impervious to the solvents used.

HINGING THE SCREEN

Whatever the surface, the screen must be hinged to it in such a way that it is easily removed. This is very necessary if a table is used or if several screens will be used on the same surface (as in multicolor printing).

And hot water sprays—used to remove a stencil or block-out—cannot be used unless the screen is first removed from its printing surface.

Two types of hinges available at hardware stores work very well—the slip pin hinge and the loose pin hinge (Figure 1.13). The loose pin hinge has a pin that, when removed, allows the two halves of the hinge to be separated. The slip pin hinge separates by sliding the two halves apart. When the slip pin hinge is used, a stop must be set up to prevent the hinge from coming apart during printing.

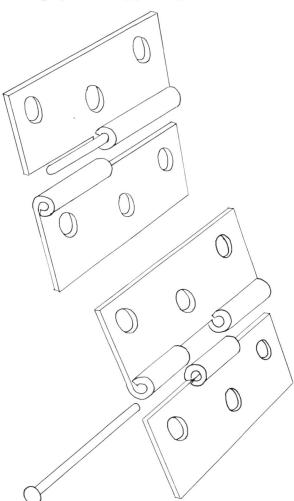

1.13 Two types of commonly used hinges.

Clamp hinges, available from screen suppliers, permit quick and easy interchangeability of screens, but they do not provide for registration of successive screens (Figure 1.14). In addition, unless these hinges

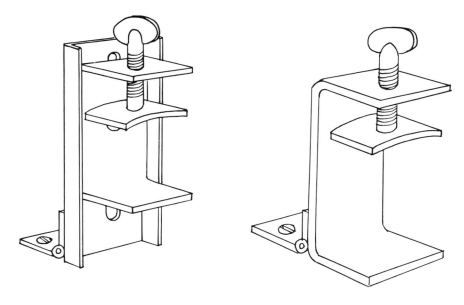

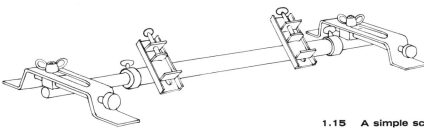

1.14 Two types of clamp hinges. The one on the left permits elevation of the screen for off-contact printing or for printing on thick stock.

1.15 A simple screen carriage.

are mortised into the printing surface, the back edge of the screen will be about ⅛ inch from the printing surface. The alternative is to build up the printing surface with Masonite, to insure full contact; for off-contact printing, however, merely insert two round-head screws on the underside of the front corners of the screen.

Screen carriages (Figure 1.15) allow rapid screen changes as well as very accurate changes in screen position after clamping.

Vacuum tables, essential to accurate registration, high volume, and large-scale work, hold the paper in perfect position during printing. This is most critical with off-contact printing, where the action of the squeegee may shift the paper. Many units have automatic switches for the vacuum, activated by raising and lowering the screen. A vacuum table keeps the paper from sticking to the screen, prevents accidents and screen clogging, and reduces printing time.

THE SQUEEGEE

The final piece of basic equipment is the squeegee. It is essentially a rubber or rubberlike blade held in a wooden or metal handle. The composition chosen for the blade will depend on the application. Traditionally, it has been black neoprene rubber. The disadvantages of this material are that it is mildly affected by most solvents in inks and abrades rapidly during printing, so requiring continual sharpening, and it may streak light colors with the dissolved particles. A better choice is tan or gray neoprene, which is less affected by solvents and will not discolor inks. Neoprene blades, of any sort, harden with age, which causes problems if the printing situation requires a specific hardness.

Newer materials—which stay sharp longer, are completely resistant to solvents, do not streak prints, and do not harden with age—are more expensive than neoprene but worth the money. Sold under various trade names, all are referred to as plastic blades.

EQUIPMENT, MATERIALS, AND SUPPLIES **19**

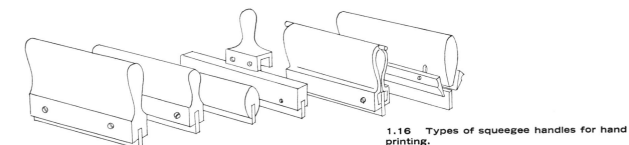

1.16 **Types of squeegee handles for hand printing.**

Squeegee blades vary in hardness, which is measured in durometers. Most work on paper and flat, smooth materials requires a medium hard, or 60-durometer, blade. On soft or highly textured materials a softer blade of 30 to 40 durometers is used. Very fine half-tone work requiring a very thin deposit of ink may demand a very hard blade of 70 to 80 durometers.

The mesh of the fabric will influence the choice of hardness in a blade. A coarse mesh requires a softer blade, a fine mesh a harder one. The desired thickness of the ink deposit is another factor in the selection of blade hardness. When thick ink deposits are wanted, a soft blade should be used. The consistency of the ink is a third factor. A stiffer ink requires a harder blade.

The handle of the squeegee should suit you. Contoured handles, of various sizes, can be used with two hands. One-handed handles come with or without a vertical handle (Figure 1.16). Adjustable handles permit changing the amount of blade exposed, so altering its flexibility.

Squeegees are usually made to order and are constructed to permit easy removal of the blade. Though blade and handle can be purchased separately, it is

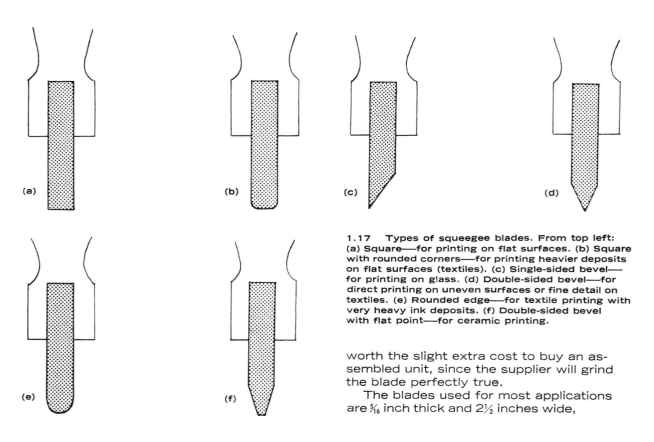

1.17 **Types of squeegee blades. From top left: (a) Square**—for printing on flat surfaces. **(b) Square with rounded corners**—for printing heavier deposits on flat surfaces (textiles). **(c) Single-sided bevel**—for printing on glass. **(d) Double-sided bevel**—for direct printing on uneven surfaces or fine detail on textiles. **(e) Rounded edge**—for textile printing with very heavy ink deposits. **(f) Double-sided bevel with flat point**—for ceramic printing.

worth the slight extra cost to buy an assembled unit, since the supplier will grind the blade perfectly true.

The blades used for most applications are $\frac{5}{16}$ inch thick and $2\frac{1}{2}$ inches wide, though other dimensions are available, usually for specialty applications. And their shape is square-cut—unless another shape is requested for special purposes (Figure 1.17).

Blades must be kept sharp and free from nicks and warping. To sharpen them yourself, tack or glue a strip of coarse flint or garnet paper to an end of a table. Hold the squeegee vertically and run it back and forth against the paper. A guide can also be built and the squeegee rested against it as it is passed back and forth (Figure 1.18).

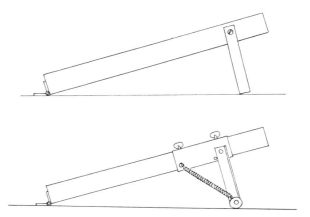

1.19   Simple screen supports.

freely. Some supports come with a spring attachment that automatically raises the screen when the squeegee is lifted. Others

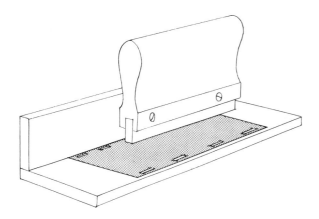

1.18   A simple squeegee sharpening guide.

A coat or two of shellac or lacquer on wooden handles will make them easier to keep clean, but do not do this if lacquer or plastic inks will be used. Store the squeegees so that the blades do not make contact with any object or surface by drilling holes in the handles and hanging them on a nail.

The squeegee blade should be 1 or 2 inches longer than the stencil is wide. This permits printing with a single stroke of the squeegee.

PRINTING ASSISTS

Various devices can speed up printing or make it easier or more accurate. Aside from those already discussed, the simplest and most useful is a wooden screen support that holds the screen in an elevated position between prints (Figure 1.19). It is usually 6 to 8 inches long and attached to one side of the frame so that it swings

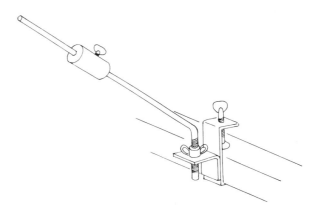

1.20   A counterbalance screen lift and support. It attaches to the back edge of screen.

have a counterbalance that either holds the screen in any position or automatically raises it to a certain height (Figure 1.20).

Squeegee carriages consist of a clamp for the squeegee that is mounted on a bar attached to the printing surface behind the screen. They will hold the squeegee at the proper angle and position during the printing stroke (Figure 1.21).

Screen blocks can be mounted on either side of the screen to ensure that it comes down precisely in the same position for each print. If there is play in the hinges, these blocks help to eliminate registration problems caused by a shifting screen (Figure 1.22).

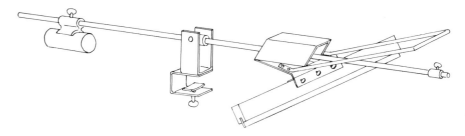

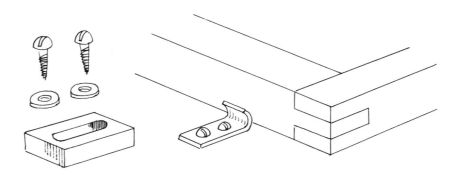

1.22   Two types of screen blocks. These should be used with slip pin hinges.

PRINT DRYING EQUIPMENT

If you make prints only occasionally or do just a few or very small ones, you may be able to do without any special provision for drying them. However, it is always easier and more convenient if some arrangement is made to speed the drying.

The simplest drying rack consists of hanging spring-loaded wooden clothespins on a cord or wire that is strung across the room (Figure 1.23). An arrangement that accommodates more prints in a smaller area requires drilling holes through the clothespins and stringing them on parallel wires (Figure 1.24). Knots can be tied in the cord to keep the clothespins apart so that prints can be placed very close together.

A drying rack, preferred by some because it can be put away easily when not

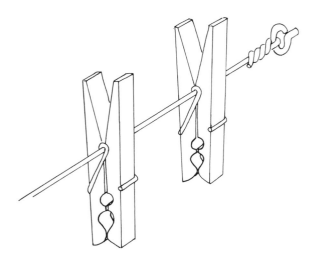

1.23   A simple clothespin and wire arrangement for drying prints.

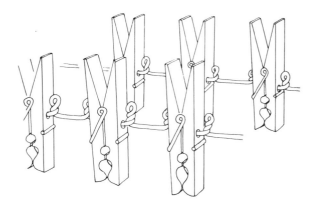

1.24   Arrangement in which clothespins have been drilled and strung on two parallel wires. Note that wires have been twisted to keep clothespins uniformly spaced.

in use, is the pallet rack. It consists of a series of wooden frames that stack one upon the other. Each can hold one or more prints, depending on their size. Frames can be built easily to any size desired (Figure 1.25).

Large portable racks are also available for those who plan very large production. These differ from the pallet rack in that each pallet is hinged at one side, permitting each in turn to be swung up out of the way.

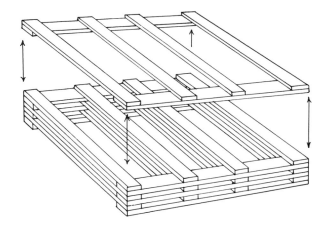

1.25   Simple pallet-type drying rack.

2. inks, vehicles, varnishes, and other materials

Many different inks are available for silk-screen printing. Some can be used for a number of different applications; others are intended for very specific uses. In most cases, the decision of which ink to use in a given situation is made early in the process. The choice will obviously relate to the idea at hand and to the surface to be printed. When paper only is considered, the decision is fairly easy, and a wide variety of inks is available for use. With materials such as glass, plastic, metal, and fabric more consideration must be given to the choice of ink. Also, the choice of ink will influence or determine the stencil to be used with it.

INK TYPES

Basically, the inks for printing fall into four distinct categories: (1) evaporation inks—ethyl cellulose, nitrocellulose, acrylic, vinyl, and some other types of plastic inks; (2) oxidation inks—enamels and synthetic enamels; (3) thermosetting inks—plastisol and hot inks; and (4) catalytic inks—epoxy and certain polymer inks.

EVAPORATION INKS

The largest group of inks, evaporation inks dry by solvent evaporation, getting harder with age and undergoing no chemical change while drying. As a result they can be redissolved or rewetted with their original solvent.

Ethyl cellulose inks are the most common general purpose inks for printing on paper, cardboard, Masonite, and wood. They are most often referred to as "screen process" or "poster" inks. These inks can be thinned with mineral spirits, kerosene, or xylol. Most often they have a flat or satin finish. The gloss types never have as high a gloss as do lacquers or enamels. They dry fairly rapidly (depending on the choice of thinner), within twenty to thirty minutes under normal conditions. No special equipment or conditions are necessary.

Any fabric, mesh or stencil can be used to print these inks.

The nitrocellulose inks, generally referred to as "lacquers," are thinned with lacquer thinner solvents. Their finishes range from satin to high gloss. They dry somewhat less rapidly than ethyl cellulose inks, requiring between thirty and sixty

minutes to become tack-free. No special conditions are required for drying.

These inks are most often used for the printing of decals, and they can also be printed on metals, foils, and some plastics. Any screen fabric can be used, but usually the meshes range from 12xx to 16xx in silk or dacron. When using monofilaments, somewhat finer meshes can be used. The stencils used must be lacquerproof, such as water-soluble or photo stencils.

Plastic inks are generally used only for the family of plastics recommended by the name or manufacturer of the ink. Of the plastic inks the vinyls are the most numerous, because of the wide use of vinyl plastics, the variation in their types and applications, and the need for excellent compatibility between ink and plastic. There are also special plastic inks for printing on mylar, polyethylene, acetate, and acrylics, to name just a few.

Of all the plastic inks, the acrylic resin inks are the most versatile. They print well on a variety of plastics because the solvent thinner for the inks is compatible with acetates, polystyrenes, and some vinyls, as well as with acrylic plastics themselves. Many of the acrylic inks are used in situations in which the printed plastic will be heat-formed later.

Practically all plastic inks dry by solvent evaporation. Some bond to the plastic chemically through solvent action, others bond only mechanically. All require specific solvents and thinners recommended by the manufacturer.

Although any screen fabric can be used with plastic inks, monofilaments are generally preferred because of easier ink passage with less build-up in the screen. Mesh requirements for multifilaments range from 10xx to 16xx; monofilaments may be finer. Lacquerproof stencils must be used.

OXIDATION INKS

Oxidation inks primarily include the enamels and the synthetic enamels. As the name implies, they undergo a chemical change during drying that renders them insoluble in their original solvent or thinner.

They offer higher gloss and greater durability than evaporation inks and can be printed on a very wide range of materials, with excellent adhesion to metals, foils, glass, some plastics, wood, cardboard, Masonite, and paper.

They dry more slowly than evaporation

inks, requiring two hours to overnight to air-dry. Commercially, hot air-drying is employed.

Although any kind of fabric may be used, monofilaments are preferred because of better ink passage and less build-up in the screen. Meshes between 10xx and 16xx (or the equivalent) are commonly used. Any kind of stencil may be used with these inks. They are commonly thinned with mineral spirits or similarly compatible solvents.

THERMOSETTING INKS

All thermosetting inks require heat in order to set or dry completely. They never become tack-free through air-drying. They are used when great durability is required or when a superior mechanical bond is needed on metals, glass, or plastics. Plastisol inks are used to print synthetic fabrics because the heat treatment fuses the ink with the fibers, becoming completely washable.

Although some of these inks may also be oxidation or catalytic inks, they are considered as a separate category because of the need for heat-drying.

One ink, "hot ink," requires an electrically heated metal screen to melt the ink to the proper consistency for printing.

Thermosetting inks will not be of much use for printing on paper and most other materials. However, if materials are to include metal or glass, and if the image requires extreme durability, then this group of inks will be most appropriately used. Many people, however, find that enamels serve just as well and do not require a heat-drying system.

CATALYTIC INKS

Most catalytic inks are epoxy types that require the addition of a catalyst just prior to printing. The inks do not dry, but cure (polymerize) as a result of the catalytic action.

With most, no heat is necessary, but it is often employed to drive off volatile solvents, speed the final hardening, and reduce the tackiness of the surface. And for certain brands, in which the catalyst is premixed with the ink, heat-curing is necessary to activate the catalyst.

These inks, like the thermosetting inks, will rarely be used by the artist. They are used when maximum durability, adhesion, and resistance to chemicals are required.

OTHER PRINTABLE MATERIALS

CERAMIC VEHICLES

Ceramic vehicles are not inks in the conventional sense. They are not pigmented inks, but vehicles carrying a glaze. After this vehicle is printed, it burns out cleanly, leaving only the fired glaze. Suppliers of silkscreen materials do not sell prepared glaze inks, but only the necessary vehicles for grinding and printing them.

Most people do not realize the extent to which silkscreen is used in ceramic decoration. Practically every piece of commercial ceramic ware is decorated by silkscreen. Plates and other flat pieces are screened directly with specially shaped screens and squeegees. For complicated surfaces or very fragile ware, special decals are printed and then affixed to the piece before firing.

TEXTILE INKS

The printing of textiles used to be far more complicated than it is today. Then it required the carrying of the dyestuff in a special vehicle that would not affect the dye and that could be removed after printing. The dyes had to be chemically treated to set and become washable and colorfast.

Modern textile plants do not rely heavily on dyeing anymore. Instead they use newly developed pigmented textile inks that have much the same quality and appearance as traditional dyes. The big advantage is the elimination of both the chemical treatment and the need for immediate heat-curing or washing.

Plastisol inks are special plastic inks that fuse with synthetic fibers upon application of heat. Some textile inks dry by evaporation, others by oxidation.

Although the stencil requirements vary with the type of textile ink, most inks can be printed with any kind of stencil. Screen fabrics of any kind can be used and a wide range of meshes are suitable, the choice depending on the type of material being printed and how much ink is to be deposited.

VARNISHES

A wide variety of varnishes, clear coats, and so on are available for special applications. Overprint varnishes are used as protective coatings over other printed inks. Binding varnishes are used for adhesion between two incompatible materials, such as in beading, flocking, and laminating. And clear decal lacquers are used to give a tough elastic film to a decal.

A varnish is selected for its compatibility with the inks previously used, drying time, clarity and finish. Most varnishes can be printed with any type of stencil (except decal lacquers) or fabric. Monofilaments are preferred because the inherent tackiness of the varnishes tends to load up and clog multifilaments. Generally, fairly coarse screens, such as 8xx or the equivalent, are used, although this is not absolutely imperative.

ETCHING AND PLATING RESISTS

In the manufacture of printed circuits a number of materials are silkscreened. Etching, plating, and solder resists are used frequently. Each is designed to print easily and accurately, and to clean up easily, but to be unaffected by the solutions and chemicals that it will later come in contact with.

Plating resists are used when circuits are electroplated onto a nonconductive substrate. Etching resists are used in the etching of printed electronic circuits. Solder resists are used when molten solder will flow over a substrate to produce a circuit.

Of the three, the etching resist is of most value to the artist since it makes it possible to translate the effects obtainable with silkscreen into an intaglio plate. (For a more detailed discussion see p. 140.)

METALLIC INKS

Although not specifically a separate category of inks, metallic inks differ somewhat from ordinary pigmented inks in their preparation.

Metallic inks use finely powdered metal in place of a pigment. The powdered metal and a vehicle are purchased separately, their type and nature being determined by the final application. Metallic inks never achieve the high polish of metal; instead, they have a dull, burnished effect similar to other metallic paints.

A specialty metallic ink used in the printing of electronic circuits is a conductive silver ink.

GLASS ETCH

Most supply catalogs now list at least one type of material suitable for etching glass. Although these screenable etches do not produce the deep, coarse etch associated with hydrofluoric etches, they do create a pronounced frosting of the glass.

These materials are safe to handle and can be used with any screen fabric or mesh. Coarser meshes will deposit a heavier amount of etch with a more pronounced effect on the glass. Stencils must be waterproof.

INK COLORS

Modern inks are formulated to very high standards. Colors are fairly consistent from batch to batch within a company, but unlike artist's oil colors, there is no standard for ink colors or for their names. Quite often the same name will be used by different manufacturers for slightly different colors, or they will have different names for the same color. When selecting and buying inks, a manufacturer's color chart is essential.

FLUORESCENT COLORS

Although most pigments in use today have good lightfastness properties, fluorescent or day-glow colors are, with few exceptions, notorious for their tendency to fade with exposure to light.

Day-glow colors in prints are more often added to the conventional colors to enhance the brilliance of a color without making it garish.

INK FORMULATION AND MODIFICATION

Since the inks used most by artists are the ethyl cellulose evaporation poster inks, our discussion of ink formulation and modification will be limited to them. For the most part it is possible to generalize to other types of inks as well. What will vary with other types will be the nature of the components and the relative proportions.

Most inks have four principal ingredients: the pigment, the vehicle, the extender, and the solvent.

The pigment is the substance that gives

color to the ink. Most pigments used today are ground very finely and uniformly. Since they are manufactured colors, they tend to be exceedingly stable.

The vehicle disperses and carries the pigment. The vehicle used depends on the type of ink. Most screen process or poster inks have a varnishlike material of ethyl cellulose. Lacquers have a nitrocellulose vehicle. Enamels have alkyd resins or linseed oils.

The extender gives the ink the body or substance necessary for printing. Usually aluminum stearate is ground in the appropriate solvent for that ink. Extenders do not alter the quality of the colors, although they do flatten the finish and reduce the luminosity of the ink.

The solvent thins the vehicle and the extender. The vehicle determines which solvent is used. Ethyl cellulose inks are soluble in mineral spirits and similar mild solvents. Lacquers require lacquer thinners. Linseed oil enamels require turpentine. Alkyd resin (synthetic) enamels use mineral spirits.

Dryers, as a rule, are not added to screen inks. The speed of drying is controlled by the solvent.

As a rule the inks come in a heavier form than is suitable for printing through a 12xx or equivalent mesh. This is particularly true for most ethyl cellulose inks intended for printing on paper. As a result some dilution or thinning with a solvent will be necessary.

Further, with most inks, there is greater pigment saturation than is necessary to print opaquely over light colors. Since extenders and vehicles purchased separately are cheaper than inks, it usually is desirable to add one or both to the ink first and then to thin it with the appropriate solvent.

Extenders serve another function besides giving body to the ink. The lubricity of the ink is increased when they are added, ensuring good passage of the ink through the screen with minimal clogging. For the poster inks commonly used by artists for printing on paper, the extender is called transparent base.

The vehicle, on the other hand, tends to increase the tackiness of the ink and to inhibit the passage of the ink through the screen, especially with multifilament fabrics.

If an ink has the consistency of heavy paste, the addition of a vehicle alone is usually sufficient. If it is a heavy liquid, the addition of transparent base is recommended.

Not all pigments have the same degree of opacity. Cool yellows tend to be transparent by nature. Blues tend to be opaque. As a result, different colors will withstand different degrees of dilution before they lose their opacity or hiding power.

Pigment Chart

color	hiding power	% transparent base that can be added
whites	fair	5–20
cool, light yellows	poor to fair	5–10
warm, dark yellows	fair to good	10–20
cool, carmine reds	fair to good	10–20
warm, fire reds	good	20
light blues	good	20
dark blues	good to excellent	20–30
blacks	excellent	30–40

The above percentages generally apply to flat poster inks being reduced with transparent base and thinned with mineral spirits. The percentage of reduction will vary, of course, depending on the brand of ink, the type of ink, the type of printing stock, and the thickness of the ink deposit.

COLOR MIXING

All ethyl cellulose inks are compatible with one another regardless of the brand or whether they are flat or gloss. Although not all manufacturers or catalogs mention this, all evaporation inks that are thinned with mineral spirits are intermixable.

When mixing and matching colors, first work with a small quantity on white paper with a palette knife. This way you can determine the approximate proportions. Save these samples. They become a valuable record for future use.

Once you have achieved your color, mix the inks in a quantity necessary for the print. Test this new mixture by spreading a portion thinly on paper and allowing it to dry. Compare it edge to edge with the original sample.

When the two match, the transparent base and solvent necessary to achieve proper printing consistency can be added (see below).

PREPARING THE INK FOR PRINTING

To the chosen or mixed color, first add the necessary amount of transparent base or vehicle and mix thoroughly. Then add the solvent to achieve the desired consistency. If the transparent base is extremely heavy, it is best to reduce it with the appropriate solvent before adding it to the ink. The mixed ink should be smooth, uniform, free from lumps or streaks of separate color.

With ethyl cellulose inks the solvent is determined by the drying speed desired. The inks come thinned with mineral spirits, and for moderate drying time mineral spirits can be used as a solvent. However, if you are just beginning silkscreen, are a slow printer, or are working under very dry conditions, you may need to lengthen the drying time. Each manufacturer provides retarder thinners for this purpose, but a good quality kerosene will work just as well. If you need to speed up the drying time, use a reducer thinner or xylol.

When using nitrocellulose inks, most enamels and synthetic enamels, and plastic inks, use the additives, diluents, extenders, and thinners recommended by the manufacturer or supplier, unless you are able to determine specific generic substitutes.

TRANSPARENT COLOR AND INKS

In the preparation of opaque inks, start with your color and add 10 percent or more of extender or modifier. With transparent colors start with a volume of vehicle and add 10 percent more or less ink, depending on how transparent you wish the color to be.

With any very transparent color, a clear base, sometimes called a toner base, crystal clear or metallic clear, should be used as the vehicle. Add 10 to 20 percent transparent base to this vehicle for body and lubricity. Thinner is added to control the drying time and to achieve the desired printing consistency. To this mixture 5 percent ink is added to obtain the desired transparent color.

For moderately transparent colors where there is a good proportion of ink, the use of transparent base alone as a vehicle will work fine.

Use of straight transparent base in place of a vehicle for very transparent colors causes dull and granular-looking color. The transparent base and solvent make a poor substitute for the vehicle, because the pigment tends to clump.

To ensure uniform mixing of the color and the vehicle, first mix a small quantity of the vehicle with the ink before combining it with the bulk of the vehicle. This can be done by working the ink and vehicle together with a palette knife on a glass or Formica surface.

Since with very transparent colors you are using the ink only for its color, other color sources can be used as well. Dry pigments, artist's oil colors, and toner colors can be used with a mixture of vehicle, transparent base, and solvent.

INK CONSISTENCY

The term most often used to describe the proper consistency is a "heavy liquid." A properly prepared opaque ink should be neither watery nor buttery. When scooped up, it should hesitate a moment before flowing back in a continuous stream. As it falls back, it should not pile up on the surface, but should level out fairly quickly.

There are, however, certain factors that will cause or require the ink to be slightly different in consistency. They are (1) the desired thickness of the ink deposit; (2) the mesh of the screen fabric; (3) the amount of transparent base or vehicle used; and (4) the type of ink used.

When thicker deposits are desired, a heavier ink is used. The consistency described above works best with a 12xx to 16xx mesh. Since the transparent base thickens the ink, an ink with a great quantity of transparent base may be considerably stiffer than our description. And when a varnish or crystal clear is added in place of an extender, the ink may be thinner than described, to overcome its tackiness.

Flat ethyl cellulose inks print well with the consistency described, but the gloss types, as well as lacquers, enamels, and plastic inks, may need to be thinned to compensate for their tackiness.

STORAGE OF INKS

For safety's sake all inks should be stored in sealable metal cans. For convenience's sake the container should also have a wide mouth and straight sides.

For small quantities, soup cans with plastic snap-top lids make good mixing and storage containers. One-pound coffee cans with plastic lids are good for larger quantities. Glass jars——because they are breakable——should be avoided, but they are preferable to plastic containers. Most plastic containers that are available in the home are made of polystyrene or polyvinyl chloride and should not be used. When inks are stored in them, these containers dissolve very slowly, ruining the ink and ultimately leaking. The only plastic that can be used safely with any ink is polyethylene, since it is resistant to all solvents.

For instant mixing and use, paper cups can be used as temporary containers, but inks cannot safely be stored in them. Moreover, the paper breathes, causing rapid evaporation of the solvent.

3.
solvents,

thinners, chemicals,

and cleaners

When I first became interested in silk-screen printing, a primary attraction was the need for very few chemicals or solvents, and those few were readily available. This was not entirely the case, as I later discovered, and it is not true today. With the proliferation of new and modified ink formulations and new and better stencil and block-out materials, there developed a need for more and more carefully tailored thinners, solvents, and chemicals. Nevertheless, to a large degree, one can still do quite well with a minimum of chemicals, using, wherever possible, those that are multipurpose.

Although ethyl cellulose inks are still those most commonly used by artists and industry, the discussion here will include chemicals that are essential to or encountered by someone using a variety of stencil techniques and inks. For the requirements of specific, specialized inks, consult your local silkscreen supplier.

ACETIC ACID

In its common dilution (5 percent), acetic acid is known as white vinegar. This non-flammable substance neutralizes the enzyme cleaners used in removing gelatin photo stencil emulsions and "preps" nylon fabrics for use with photo stencils. It is also used with isopropyl alcohol or water as an adhering fluid for certain water-soluble stencils.

ACETONE

Acetone is available at many hardware and drug stores and is commonly used as a nail polish remover. A principal ingredient in lacquer thinners, this highly flammable chemical is used to remove stubborn spots of lacquer stencil, ink, or direct emulsion from screen fabric.

ALCOHOLS

Three alcohols readily available at hardware and drug stores are frequently used in silkscreen.

Ethyl alcohol (ethanol, grain alcohol, denatured alcohol) is used for thinning or removing shellac. It is also used with the water in glue-resist stencils to accelerate the drying time. In certain brands of commercial water-soluble block-out it is a component of the thinner.

Isopropyl alcohol (rubbing alcohol) is available at any drugstore in either 70 or 99 percent strength. It is frequently used

with vinegar or water as an adhering fluid for some types of water-soluble stencils or as a wetting and drying agent. It is also used to reduce the swelling and to speed the drying of photo stencil emulsions.

Methyl alcohol (wood alcohol, methanol) is similar in use to ethyl alcohol, but is also a component of thinner for certain brands of water-soluble block-out. It works exceptionally well for removing lacquer stencils from the screen.

AMMONIUM BICHROMATE

A light-sensitive chemical, ammonium bichromate is used in the sensitization of many photo stencils. It is somewhat more light sensitive than potassium bichromate. It is available in either powdered or granular form at many large photography stores or from silkscreen suppliers. It has a fairly long shelf life if stored away from moisture, light, and heat.

BENZENE

A highly flammable substance, benzene can be used for screen wash-up, but its principal use is as a rubber cement thinner.

BUTYL CELLOSOLVE

A flammable chemical, butyl cellosolve is used as a mild lacquer solvent and as a retarder in certain enamels and other inks. It is not generally available except through chemical supply houses or larger silkscreen suppliers, but it, and its companion, cellosolve, are excellent ink removers. Remove the oldest and most stubborn ink by soaking the screen, brushes, and tools overnight and washing them out with soap and water the next day.

CHLORINE BLEACH

Certain direct photographic emulsions are removed from synthetic screen fabrics by using household chlorine bleach full strength. It should not be used on silk fabrics because it destroys the fabric. Chlorine bleach is nonflammable.

ENZYME CLEANERS

All suppliers and manufacturers have their own enzyme cleaners, but for practical purposes they are interchangeable. Their principal function is to remove gelatin photo stencils from the screen. Many emulsions are not soluble in water until converted to a soluble form by the action of the enzyme.

ETHYLENE DICHLORIDE

A highly flammable chemical, ethylene dichloride is used in combination with methyl alcohol to thin certain brands of water-soluble block-out and to remove stubborn spots of lacquer stencil and block-out from the screen.

HYDROGEN PEROXIDE

Nonflammable hydrogen peroxide is commonly used in very dilute strengths as a developer for a variety of presensitized photo stencil materials. It is available from silkscreen suppliers at twenty volume, six percent, or at the drugstore at three percent strength.

ISOPHORONE

Isophorone is a flammable solvent thinner used in thinning vinyl-based inks and plating or acid resists. It is available from silkscreen suppliers as specialized thinners or from chemical suppliers.

KEROSENE

Commonly available at hardware stores and many gas stations, kerosene is used as a retarder thinner—to slow down the drying time of ethyl cellulose inks. Various grades are available, but the canned kerosene from hardware stores is best. Kerosene is flammable.

KITCHEN CLEANSERS

Most kitchen cleansers consist of fine pumice particles, a soap, and, unfortunately, chlorine bleach. The fine particulate cleansers without bleach can be used for degreasing screens in preparation for photo stencils. Pumice bar soaps can also be used.

LACQUER THINNERS

Since lacquer thinners are a combination of several solvents (acetone, toluol, alcohol, xylol, etc.), they vary widely from brand to brand. Generally they are categorized as fast, medium, or slow thinners.

Manufacturers of lacquer stencil film recommend the slow types for adhering their films and the fast types for stencil removal. Most brands available at hardware stores do not indicate their speed, but are generally a medium speed, often suitable for both adhesion and removal of lacquer stencils.

Lacquer thinners are compatible with lacquer (nitrocellulose) inks and are used for thinning and wash-up. Many evaporation plastic inks (modified acrylics) require lacquer thinner as a wash-up.

Manufacturers of stencils tend to recommend their brands of adhering fluids because they are tailored to their materials. Although their cost is greater, their results are predictably better.

It is advisable when using common thinners for adhesion to experiment with scraps of stencil to determine whether they work satisfactorily. Lacquer thinners are highly flammable.

METHYL CHLORIDE

Methyl chloride, which is highly flammable, is similar to ethylene dichloride, but is used in combination with ethyl alcohol to thin some brands of water-soluble block-out. It is usually available only through chemical supply houses.

MINERAL SPIRITS

Mineral spirits is a readily available paint thinner and brush cleaner. This flammable substance is known by different names in various parts of the country. Oleum, varnolene, pakosol, and odorless paint thinner are some of these names. In some areas the name benzene is incorrectly used to mean mineral spirits.

Its principal use is as a thinner and wash-up for ethyl cellulose inks and some types of enamels. The various types of mineral spirits differ mainly in their flash point—the temperature at which they ignite. The lower the flash point, the more volatile a chemical it is, the more rapidly it evaporates, and the more quickly it dissolves or mixes with ink. All are interchangeable and affect only the drying time of the inks.

NAPHTHA

Naphthas are highly flammable and come in various grades depending on their flash points. They are used as a wash-up for certain specialty inks. Their most common use is as a cleaning fluid.

POLYVINYL ACETATE

A principal, and nonflammable, ingredient in direct photographic stencil emulsions, polyvinyl acetate is usually combined with polyvinyl alcohol. When treated with a bichromate salt, it becomes light sensitive. Unsensitized it has a long shelf life, but once sensitized it must be used within twenty-four hours. It is readily available from silkscreen suppliers under different trademarks.

POLYVINYL ACRYLIC

Polyvinyl acrylic is a principal ingredient in acrylic paints and many white glues. It is used in silkscreen to lift printed images from clay coated papers to make positives suitable for photo stencils. In experiments it has been used as a direct photo emulsion, but it is difficult to remove from the screen.

Polyvinyl acrylic is readily available from art supply stores as an acrylic polymer painting medium with a matte or gloss finish. Shelf life is long if it is stored in well-sealed plastic containers. It is nonflammable.

POLYVINYL ALCOHOL

A flammable, water-soluble form of polyvinyl, polyvinyl alcohol is used frequently as a mold release in plastic casting. It is also used in combination with polyvinyl acetate in direct photographic emulsions. It is readily available from silkscreen suppliers in a form suitable for direct-emulsion coatings. Its shelf life is excellent if it is stored in well-sealed plastic containers.

POTASSIUM BICHROMATE

A light-sensitive chemical used to sensitize many photo stencil materials, potassium bichromate is less sensitive than ammonium bichromate. It is purchased in either powdered or granular form and is dissolved in water to produce a sensitizing solution that is then added to the emulsion.

Its shelf life is good if it is stored away from moisture, light, and heat. It is readily available from silkscreen suppliers. Potassium bichromate is nonflammable.

TALCUM POWDER

Talcum powder is used to dry and harden lithographic crayon or tusche used with direct-drawn resist stencils. It is readily available in scented form and is not necessarily white. However, neither its color nor its scent is significant.

TOLUOL

Toluol is a highly flammable ingredient in lacquer thinners. It is used with lacquer inks as a wash-up.

TRISODIUM PHOSPHATE

Once a principal ingredient in laundry detergents, trisodium phosphate is now available only through silkscreen suppliers. It is used in screen preparation as a degreasing agent to remove old traces of ink residue and to ensure good adhesion of photographic stencils. It is nonflammable.

TURPENTINE

Although several different kinds of turpentine are available, these flammable chemicals are not used in commercial silkscreen printing because of their cost. However, for the artist who does not have professional screen-washing equipment at his disposal, turpentine is superior to other solvents for removing ethyl cellulose or enamel inks from the screen.

Although it is not as volatile as some grades of mineral spirits, benzene, or naphtha, its ability to break down paint and pigment particles and carry them out of the screen makes it an excellent and rapid cleaning agent. As a result, a smaller amount of turpentine is needed to clean a screen than is required with mineral spirits, naphtha, or benzene. Mineral spirits tends to flow out of the screen, leaving the ink behind. This necessitates a constant flood of mineral spirits and a great deal of mopping up. Naphtha and benzene tend to evaporate before the dissolved ink can be removed, requiring use of much more of the solvent.

Three turpentines are generally available at hardware and paint stores: wood sulfite, steam-distilled, and gum turpentines, and all are equally effective.

With the recent rise in the cost of turpentine, some manufacturers have come out with turpentine substitutes. One of these is Nankee's ST 100. It works and smells like turpentine, but is cheaper.

There are also three turpentines that should be avoided. Subturps is a low-grade end product that tends to leave a sticky residue in the screen. Venice turpentine is exceedingly expensive and too thick to be used as a cleaner. Artist's rectified turpentine is the elite of turpentines, being the purest, but it is prohibitively expensive.

When using any turpentine to clean a screen, it is important to wipe the screen thoroughly dry when finished and to not permit it to air-dry. This will minimize the build-up of turpentine residue in the screen and will prolong the life and usefulness of the fabric. What little residue does accumulate can be easily removed with trisodium phosphate.

XYLOL
A highly flammable solvent, xylol is similar in its applications to toluol but acts somewhat more slowly. It is used as a thinner and wash-up for lacquer and synthetic enamel inks. It is also used as a fast thinner for ethyl cellulose inks.

WATER
The primary function of water is for thinning hide glue when used as a resist stencil or block-out and for removing glue resists, water-soluble stencils, and some photo stencils. It is also used in the development and wash-out of photo stencils.

There are many other generic solvents, thinners, and so on. However, their applications are usually so specific that they need not be covered here. Innumerable other specialized brand solvents and thinners are tailored to specific brands and types of material. They, too, are beyond the scope of this book.

3.1   Safety equipment used to handle volatile solvents. From left: plunger can, benzene can, respirator, safety can.

SAFETY
Many of these solvents are extremely flammable. Some are also exceedingly hazardous if breathed over prolonged periods of time. In particular, the chlorinated and aromatic hydrocarbons—lacquer thinners, acetone, ethylene dichloride, toluol, methyl chloride—can irreparably damage the liver and kidneys if there is prolonged exposure to them. And some, such as mineral spirits or turpentine, can cause rashes and peeling or cracking of the skin. (See Figure 3.1.)

Observe the following rules when using any solvent or thinner.

1.   Use only in well-ventilated areas. Open the windows and turn on a fan, even in winter.
2.   Avoid opening or using more than one solvent at any one time.
3.   Store all flammable materials in metal cans, and keep them in a ventilated metal cabinet.
4.   Use a metal refuse can with a metal lid to dispose of used materials and empty it at least once a day.
5.   When using any of the aromatic or chlorinated hydrocarbons, schedule your work so that you can take a break or work elsewhere until all the fumes dissipate.
6.   Do not smoke while you are using solvents, or in the area where solvents are stored.
7.   If you feel lightheaded or have a headache or lower backache, move away from all solvents and fumes for the rest of the day.
8.   If you find you cannot avoid continual exposure to fumes, invest in a good respirator with a filter rated for removal of aromatic and chlorinated hydrocarbons.
9.   If the skin of your hands is sensitive to a solvent or becomes so, use disposable polyethylene gloves.

4. knife-cut

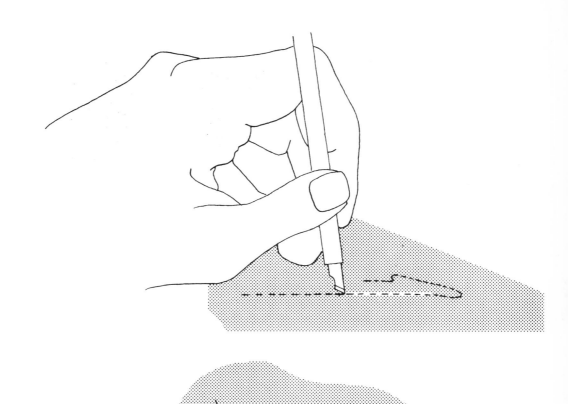

stencils

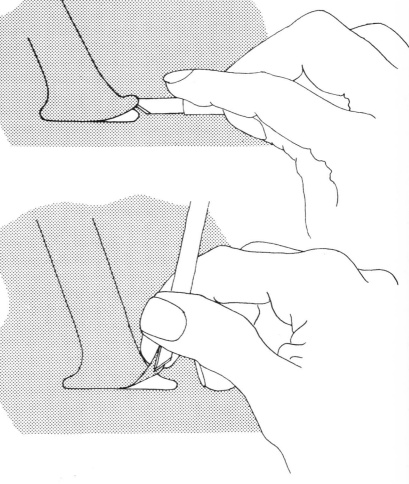

In any kind of silkscreen printing, a stencil is needed to control where the ink will and will not print on a surface. This creates the intended pattern, design or image.

Stencils are of three kinds: knife-cut, photographic, and resist. This chapter will deal with knife-cut stencil techniques.

For speed and ease of use, nothing surpasses the knife-cut stencil, though it can be exceedingly detailed and complex. As the name implies, the stencil is cut with a knife, usually a stencil or frisket knife.

The stencil material itself may be paper, lacquer-soluble film, or water-soluble film. The stencil is prepared by cutting and removing those areas that are to be printed. Prior to printing, the stencil is fastened to the screen in a fixed position. Paper stencils are held in place on the screen by the surface tension of the printing ink. The film stencils are adhered to the screen fabric by melting the film with its particular solvent and embedding it in the screen.

STENCIL CUTTING TOOLS

The basic tool is a well-sharpened stencil knife that fits comfortably in the hand and can be manipulated freely to cut fine detail, flowing curves, or straight lines. As a rule, the handle or shaft should be about the size of a pencil. The blade should come to a point, but not at too steep an angle. Too steep an angle can cause the knife to tear, puncture, or skid on the stencil. (See Figures 4.1 and 4.2.)

The blade should be kept as sharp as possible. Even new blades or knives should be sharpened before use since they are machine-ground and frequently have nicks

4.1   Good stencil knives.

4.2   Bad stencil knives.

or burrs. Although only the very tip of a knife is used, in order to maintain the best angle and sharpest point, the whole blade is sharpened.

Sharpening a knife and keeping it sharp are easy if the following rules are observed.

1.   Never use the knife for anything but cutting stencils.
2.   Never let it get so dull that it requires reshaping.
3.   Always sharpen it as if you are shaving the stone.
4.   Use a good quality oil sharpening stone (medium India) with oil.
5.   Learn to determine the sharpness of the blade by visual inspection.

When sharpening the stencil knife, it should lie with the beveled side flat on the oil stone. The knife is then pushed, as if shaving the stone. If you are not sure you have it flat, rock the blade back and forth until you can feel that it is in the correct position. Never pull the blade toward you or rotate it in a circular motion, as this will form a burr of metal on the tip that can break off, damaging the blade. When the blade is pushed, the metal is ground under the blade and removed cleanly. (See Figure 4.3.)

Even after you have the technique down pat, you may have difficulty knowing when the blade is properly sharpened. The best and most accurate method is by visual inspection.

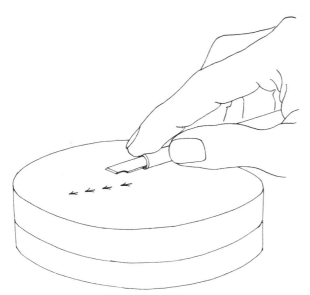

4.3 Proper sharpening technique for stencil knives.

Sit facing a light above you. Turn the knife, edge up, and aim it at the light. Look along the edge of the blade to the point. If you see a white highlight at the tip, the knife is too dull to cut easily. As practice at inspecting, take any knife you know to be dull and see if you can find the highlight. A dull knife may show only a tiny pinpoint of light at the tip. A razor-sharp knife cannot reflect light from its edge. The blade should be sharpened equally on both sides to prevent the blade from being ground down unevenly.

With a knife that has a rigid blade, it is important that the handle fit comfortably in the hand and be able to be rotated securely between the thumb and forefinger. This makes it easy to follow and cut very fine detail accurately. A large, cumbersome utility knife cannot be manipulated with any control or precision.

One of the most readily available knives is the #1 X-acto with a number eleven or sixteen blade. This knife costs under a dollar, has interchangeable blades, and is slightly larger than a pencil. Many people prefer this knife because of its heavier weight. X-acto also makes a similar knife with a smaller handle.

The cheapest knife is a fixed-blade frisket or stencil knife. This knife costs about forty cents. The blade is fixed in an aluminum or plastic shaft that is somewhat thinner than a pencil.

Many people prefer swivel knives in which the blade rotates to the proper cutting direction as the hand moves. These knives permit the cutting of full circles in one stroke without twisting the hand or the stencil around. Several types are available, and in most the blade can be locked to make long, straight cuts. Although it takes considerable practice to master the swivel knife, if you plan to do a great deal of finely detailed cutting, this knife will be easier, faster, and more accurate.

There are several specialized tools for cutting stencils. Dual or bi-line cutters are used when uniform parallel lines are desired. In Figure 4.4 the first cutter on the left has two blades that are mounted in such a way that the space between can be adjusted from $\frac{1}{16}$ to $\frac{5}{8}$ inch. This is probably the best choice when a wide variety of line widths is important.

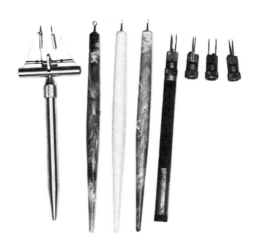

4.4 Types of bi-line cutters.

The Master Bi-Cutter has interchangeable heads with two blades in fixed positions. This knife is good for lines from $\frac{1}{16}$ to $\frac{1}{4}$ inch apart. It is difficult to move in a flowing, freehand manner because of the difficulty in keeping both blades pressing uniformly into the stencil.

The tool that gives the greatest freedom of cutting is the Ramsey Film Line Cutter. It is designed, however, for fine lines between $\frac{1}{32}$ and $\frac{1}{8}$ inch apart and each size requires a separate tool. Instead of conventional blades it has a loop of specially hardened and sharpened steel. It can be handled freely as if one were drawing with it.

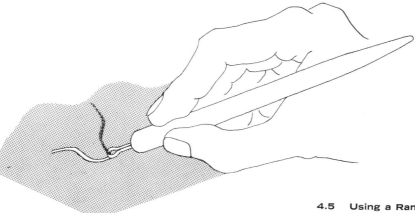

It is also self-stripping, removing the cut stencil as it cuts (Figure 4.5).

All bi-line cutters are a nuisance to sharpen because of the difficulty in getting at both sides of the two blades. The Ramsey cutter is impossible to sharpen, but because of its special construction it will remain sharp for a long time if properly cared for.

Various types of compasses for cutting circles up to 12 inches in radius are available. However, a draftsman's compass can be used with a special blade in place of the lead.

For large circles a good compass is the Master Beam Compass Cutter (Figure 4.6). This compass will cut circles up to 12

inches in radius. A particular advantage is that it will accept the Master Bi-Cutter blades, which then permit cutting concentric arcs or circles.

PAPER STENCILS

Any reasonably thin paper—tracing paper, layout bond, offset bond—can be used as a stencil. Paper has advantages over films in that it is cheap and readily available and can be fastened quickly and easily to the screen. There are, however, several disadvantages. Generally, only fairly simple stencils can be made. Maintaining precise registration of one color to another is difficult because the stencil shifts. Because paper lacks durability the edges of the stencil fray during printing. Thick papers also cause raggedness along the cut edges of the stencil (Figure 4.7). Finally, a paper stencil becomes saturated with ink during printing and cannot be salvaged for printing in other colors.

Paper stencils do allow for certain

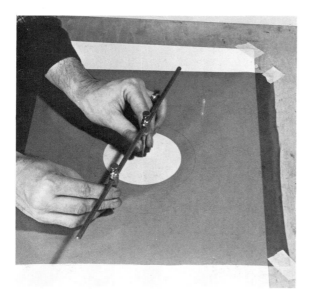

4.6   Using a Master Beam Compass Cutter.

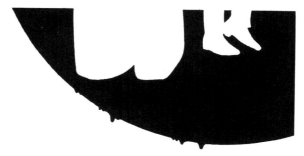

4.7   Bleeding of ink caused by thick stencil, slack screen, or wrinkled stencil.

effects that are unobtainable with solvent-adhering films. They can be torn in various ways, creating unusual edge properties. If very porous papers are used, the bleeding of the ink through the stencil will create interesting textured effects (Figure 4.8).

4.8   Some effects of tearing and bleeding, possible with paper stencils.

Paper works well with reasonably small stencils (up to 16″ x 20″), but with larger ones the shift in the screen fabric frequently causes the ink to squirt under the stencil.

CUTTING THE STENCIL
To cut a paper stencil, tape your original drawing to a smooth surface, such as a piece of chip board or oak tag cardboard, and over this tape down a piece of stencil paper that is at least two inches larger on each side than the print will be, and ideally, large enough to cover the entire screen opening. If the stencil paper is opaque, your drawing will have to be made directly on the paper.

With a well-sharpened knife cut along the edges of the shapes to be printed and remove them. If you wish to save your original drawing, trace the areas to be cut and remove the drawing before cutting. Make sure to cut through the stencil with a single stroke of the knife. When cutting corners, avoid overlapping cuts. With tracing paper in particular, these overlapped cuts may print as fine lines (Figure 4.9).

4.9   The effect of overlapped knife cuts with paper stencils.

Handle the stencil paper with care both before and after cutting it. Creasing, curling, or wrinkling the stencil may cause problems in printing. Always store the stencil in a flat position.

4.10   Poor printing along edges of shapes caused by thick stencil, thick ink, dull squeegee, etc.

ATTACHING THE STENCIL

The stencil is taped flat to the underside of the screen. Whenever possible, use masking tape only at the corners. This allows the stencil to shift and conform to the screen fabric during printing. The surface tension of the ink will be sufficient in most cases to hold the stencil firmly on the screen. When using inks that have large quantities of transparent base, it may be necessary to tape the stencil more securely.

If your stencil has several shapes that are unattached to the border of the stencil, taping at the corners will not attach these pieces. There are two ways to get them in proper position on the screen.

In the first method, lay your original drawing beneath the screen. Over this place your stencil, together with all the cut pieces, and position everything accurately. Place masking tape on the corners, sticky side up, with about one inch of tape extending (Figure 4.11). Lower the screen, press down on the silk with one hand and attach the tape by rubbing with the other (Figure 4.12). With the screen still in position, apply a drop of mucilage to the unattached pieces and press with a finger for a moment to ensure adhesion (Figure 4.13). When the screen is raised, all portions of the stencil will be in position on the screen (Figure 4.14). Use only one or two dots of glue per piece. Too much glue can result in wrinkling of shapes, causing

4.12 Attaching a stencil by pressing in center and rubbing out to tape at corners.

printing problems. The glue must be washed out with water after printing clean-up.

In the second method, the original drawing is again placed beneath the screen. A piece of tracing paper is then placed over the drawing, and the stencil is positioned on the tracing paper. The screen is then lowered carefully and printing is begun, taking care not to disturb the stencil until the first print is pulled. The surface tension

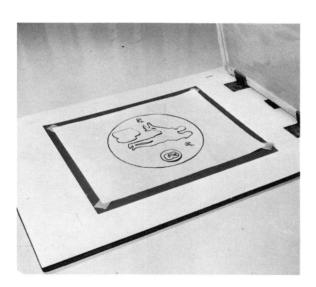

4.11 Stencil in position with tape at corners. Note that the cut-away pieces have been left in position to keep loose pieces in register.

4.13 Pressing down on a spot of glue to attach a loose piece of stencil.

4.14 Stencil attached to screen, with printing area fallen away.

of the ink holds all stencil pieces in their proper places (Figure 4.15). Tape is then applied to the outer edges of the stencil.

4.15 A paper stencil attached to the screen by ink surface tension alone.

This method does not require additional clean-up since no glue is used. However, during printing, unattached pieces tend to peel off the screen, especially when the printing ink is heavy or tacky.

STENCIL REPAIR

If a stencil becomes torn or a piece is cut away accidentally, you are probably going to have problems during printing, no matter the corrective measures taken. However, if you've invested considerable time in preparing the stencil, you may be willing to take certain risks rather than to cut it again.

If the cut is not immediately adjacent to any printing area, cellophane tape can be applied to the underside.

If the cut or tear runs off from a printing area, position cellophane tape on the underside so that as little of it as possible is adjacent to the printing area or edge (Figure 4.16). This will minimize the increased thickness along the printing edges and reduce the possibility of the ink clogging during printing.

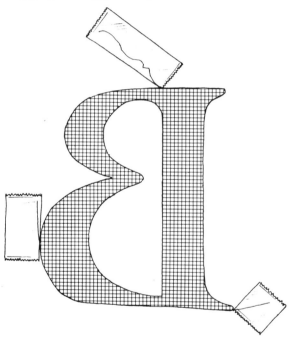

4.16 How to position cellophane tape when repairing tears and miscuts in paper stencils.

If the stencil has become creased or curled from careless handling, try ironing it with a dry iron set at a low temperature.

SPECIAL EFFECTS

Paper stencils can be used to achieve effects unique to the material, such as torn edges and absorbency. Different papers tear differently, yielding characteristic edges. The disadvantage is the lack of control in tearing stencils accurately and in close register to one another.

All papers can be made to bleed, but some more than others. Unpolished newsprint, inexpensive layout papers, and even paper toweling and lightweight ditto paper can be used. Each bleeds in a pattern or texture that is characteristic of that paper and its calender.

To achieve the desired degree of bleeding, it is necessary to thin the ink with both thinner and transparent base. Usually the screen is flooded with ink and allowed to sit until the ink appears through the paper. Printing is then begun. The prints vary considerably from one another, and the degree of bleeding tends to increase with each successive print. Generally this technique is used for very limited editions in which precision of effect and registration is not critical.

LACQUER STENCILS

The various lacquer stencil films available all work in roughly the same way. Originally these stencils were made from lacquer, hence their name. Today many are made from synthetic materials, but they are still soluble in lacquer thinner.

PAPER-BACKED LACQUER STENCILS

All lacquer stencils are composed of two parts: a thin film of lacquer-like plastic laminated with a wax adhesive to a heavier translucent backing sheet. The backing sheet keeps the pieces of the stencil in proper position during cutting and permits much greater precision than do paper stencils.

The inexpensive stencils have a paper backing sheet, but most of these tend to curl and are easily creased or kinked, creating problems both in cutting and adhesion. These films tend to be inelastic and do not cut and strip away easily. Many paper-backed stencils absorb moisture, shrinking and expanding with changes in humidity, and creating problems with close registration. When possible, only moisture-proof varieties should be used. The lacquer film on many of these stencils tends to dry out and become brittle with age, making the cutting and adhesion more difficult. Many also fade with age, completely losing their color.

PLASTIC-BACKED LACQUER STENCILS

The plastic-backed lacquer stencils are generally superior in every way. Even when stored in a roll, they will lie flat when unrolled. The properties of the film make it much easier to cut and strip away. They are less likely to dry out or fade. They have good adhesion to the backing sheet, so that pieces do not accidentally come off in the cutting. They resist creasing and kinking. They are usually more translucent, making it easier to see through several layers. They are not affected by moisture, allowing for extremely accurate registration. Finally, they tend to adhere more easily with a variety of common lacquer thinners.

STENCIL COLOR

Most brands of lacquer stencil come in three colors: amber, blue, and green. The choice is yours; I find the amber easier to see through.

SIZE AVAILABILITY

Most materials can be purchased in a variety of roll sizes. A few are also available in precut sheets. The standard roll sizes are 40″ x 150″, 40″ x 300″, 44″ x 150″, and 44″ x 300″.

CUTTING THE STENCIL

There is a major difference between cutting a paper stencil and cutting a lacquer one. Because paper is fibrous, a certain amount of pressure must be used to ensure a clean cut with a single stroke of the knife. With lacquer stencils, the film offers practically no resistance and is considerably thinner than most papers. Only the weight of the knife and the pressure necessary to drag it across the stencil are needed to cut it. Indeed, you want to cut **only** the film. You do not want to score, crease, or cut through the backing sheet. If a dull knife is used with too much pressure, the backing sheet will become indented, making it difficult to get good adhesion because of poor contact along those edges. At worst, the adhering fluid pools up in the creases and melts away the edges of shapes and fine detail.

If too much pressure is used with a sharp knife, the backing sheet will be cut through. With plastic-backed films this is

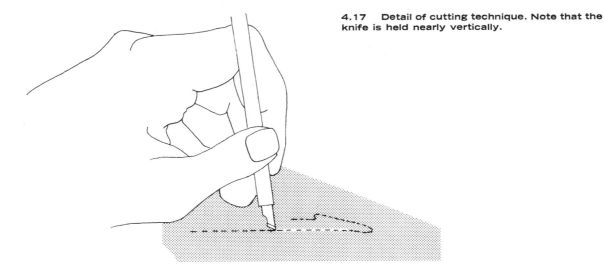

4.17 Detail of cutting technique. Note that the knife is held nearly vertically.

not serious as long as the backing sheet remains in one piece. With paper-backed films the stencil tends to curl where cut, making it difficult to get good contact during adhesion.

To prepare a lacquer stencil, first tape your drawing to a piece of cardboard or drawing board. Always cut on a smooth, flat surface that is reasonably hard. Cutting on a soft surface (a pad of news-print or paper) will almost always cause creasing of the backing sheet.

Over the sketch, tape a sheet of stencil film with the lacquer side up. It should be at least an inch larger than the drawing on all sides. Draw a very sharp stencil knife, held in a near-vertical position, along the lines to be cut, without applying any down-ward pressure (Figure 4.17). Try to hold the knife loosely. If you clench it tightly, your hand will not only cramp quickly, but you will probably start applying too much pressure without noticing it.

The best way to judge cutting pressure is to run your fingertips along the underside of the stencil periodically while cutting. If you feel bumps or creases, you are using too much pressure (Figure 4.18).

If the lighting is good, you can usually see any unevenness of the surface of your stencil if your pressure is too great. The lighting should come from slightly in front and opposite the hand that is cutting. You do not want the light to glare on the sten-cil, but you do want to be able to see which lines you have cut.

Holding the knife in a near-vertical posi-

tion will allow you to make very small, tight turns. Do not let the knife lean to one side while cutting as this will raise the edge of the stencil off the backing sheet, which, when cutting fine detail, can cause a small piece to lift off.

In contrast with paper stencil, when cutting sharp corners on lacquer stencils, always overlap your cuts. This ensures that when the printing areas are removed, the portions that are to remain will not accidentally tear or come off because of incomplete cuts.

If while cutting curves you need to lift the knife off the line before it is completed, try to place the knife back on the cut

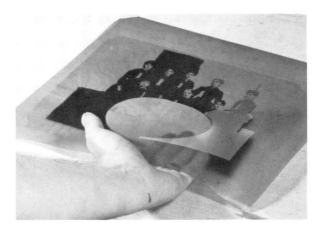

4.18 Running fingers along underside of stencil to check cutting pressure. Bumps and creases indicate too much pressure.

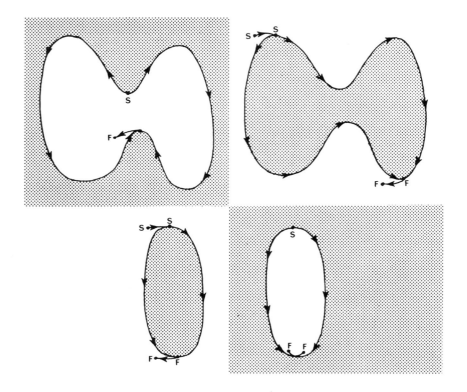

4.19 Cutting curved shapes with multiple strokes. S indicates beginning of cut; F indicates finish of cut. Note that cuts begin and end at points of maximum curvature. Shaded area represents portion of stencil not stripped away.

portion and continue cutting. If you have difficulty doing this, start your knife on the side of the line where the stencil is going to be stripped away, and join the line where you left off.

If you have to complete a curve by cutting from the opposite direction, end the first cut at a point of maximum curvature. Make the second cut to overlap the end of the first cut and end it in an area that will be stripped away (Figure 4.19).

Once a shape is completely cut, use the point of your knife to lift a corner of the stencil (Figure 4.20) enough to grasp it with your fingers or tweezers (Figure 4.21). Gently pull off the piece, watching to see that all is removed and that no adjacent area is tearing or lifting off. Put these

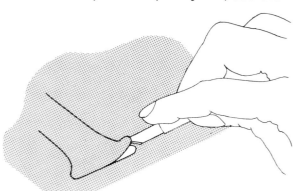

4.20 Using a stencil knife to separate a cut piece of stencil from the backing sheet.

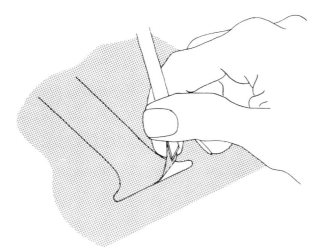

4.21 Using a knife and forefinger to strip cut piece from backing sheet.

scraps of stripped film in a jar for later use as a block-out solution (see p. 61). Generally, the better plastic-backed stencils strip out cleanly even if the film is not cut completely through. The paper-backed types must be cut completely or they may tear into nonprinting areas.

When you have completed cutting and stripping away the printing areas of the stencil, cut and strip away a ¼-inch strip along one edge. This will make removal of

To be sure that your screen is clean enough, take two pads of paper toweling saturated with lacquer thinner and scrub both sides simultaneously. If only the faintest tint appears on the pads, the screen is clean enough.

If you have been using common lacquer thinner for adhering lacquer stencils and notice a faint trace of stencil color remaining in the screen after removal, it is advisable to scrub the screen with acetone to

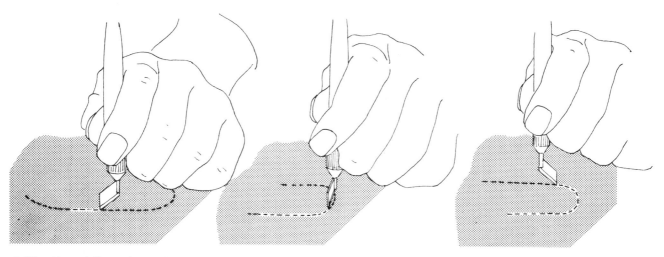

4.22   Use of the swivel knife, showing how the blade rotates as the hand changes direction.

the backing sheet easier after adhesion.

When working with a swivel knife, the cutting technique is different. Some knives must be held vertically; others can be held in a more comfortable penlike position. In any case, the knife is never rotated between the thumb and fingers, nor does the hand turn when cutting a curve. The blade itself swivels in the right direction as the hand changes direction (Figure 4.22).

SCREEN PREPARATION AND REQUIREMENTS

When the stencil is completed, it must be adhered to a screen that is thoroughly clean and in good tight condition. As a rule, lacquer stencils work best on multi-filament fabrics such as silk or dacron. Old fabrics in which the threads have become clogged with ink, stencil, or block-out residue do not adhere well.

Any mesh screen may be used, but generally 10xx to 16xx meshes are used. The finer meshes hold fine detail better and are less likely to cause sawtooth edges.

remove it. Successive stencils will become harder and harder to adhere properly if this residue is allowed to remain in the screen. (See **Adhering Fluids,** p. 50.)

ADHERING

After taping the stencil to the printing side of the screen with the lacquer film in contact with the fabric, place a piece of ¼-inch Masonite or similar material beneath the screen (Figure 4.23). This pack-up ensures tight contact between the stencil and the screen during adhesion. The pack-up should be as large as the stencil, but smaller than the inside dimensions of the screen. The pack-up should not be thicker than ¼-inch, as material that is too thick will dent the screen to such an extent that the stencil will be deformed and the backing sheet may buckle, causing problems during adhesion.

Fold paper toweling into two pads approximately 2 inches square. Saturate one pad with adhering fluid. It should be

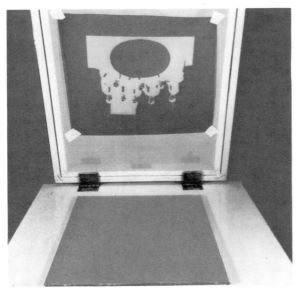

4.23 A stencil taped to the screen with pack-up below, ready for adhesion.

wet but not dripping. Starting in the center of your stencil, apply the wet pad to an area about 8 inches square (Figure 4.24). You should notice that the stencil immediately becomes darker in color. Immediately wipe up excess fluid with the dry pad (Figure 4.25). Repeat this process over the entire stencil, working from the center

to the edges. At no time use much pressure, either in applying the adhering fluid or in wiping. If the pads become stained with the stencil, refold or replace them to prevent depositing traces of stencil in the open areas of the screen. For very large stencils it is sometimes better to work from one end to the other instead of from the center out.

After the stencil has been adhered, repeat the process, but use a less saturated pad for applying the adhering fluid. This ensures good over-all adhesion and produces a thinner stencil, permitting more consistent printing of fine detail.

A Note About Adhering Fluids

Each stencil manufacturer and supplier recommends its own brand of adhering fluid, though each is essentially a type of lacquer thinner and all are interchangeable. Many brands of lacquer thinner are also available at hardware and paint stores. Some of these work well, others do not, but all are less expensive. Generally, the plastic-backed stencils work wel with a variety of common lacquer thinners, but the paper-backed varieties are more difficult. For the sake of convenience and for emergency situations when the recommended fluid may be unavailable, I would advise experimenting with the thinners that are more available.

4.24 Applying adhering fluid with a small pad of paper toweling. The darker area indicates adhesion.

4.25 Mopping up excess adhering fluid with a dry pad. Note that only a small area is worked on at one time.

BACKING SHEET REMOVAL

Because adhering fluid evaporates rapidly, the backing sheet can be removed within about ten minutes. To do this, grasp the backing sheet at a corner or along the edge where the film was stripped away (Figures 4.26 and 4.27). Pull gently and slowly, diagonally across the stencil, looking between the backing sheet and the film to see that it is coming off cleanly and that the stencil is adhered well to the screen.

4.27 Backing sheet being removed after stencil is dry. Note the piece of stencil clinging to backing sheet as a result of poor adhesion.

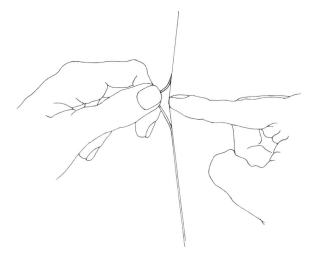

4.26 Poking from the inside of the screen to separate a corner of the backing sheet.

little thinner as possible, and finish quickly and efficiently. The best way to handle lacquer thinner is to puncture two holes in the seal of the can rather than removing the seal entirely.

Once the backing sheet is removed, run your fingers across the underside of the stencil. If the edges of some areas drag or pull up under your fingers, they need to be re-adhered. Visually inspect the stencil from the squeegee side of the screen. If some areas have become lighter, the adhesion is not good (Figure 4.28).

Place the backing sheet on the pack-up and lower the screen. Using only a dampened pad of toweling, go over those areas that are not adhered. If the problem is general, go over the entire stencil. If the problem is chronic, stencil after stencil, check to see that your adhering fluid is appropriate or that your screen is clean enough.

STENCIL REMOVAL

Methyl alcohol or any lacquer thinner can be used to remove a stencil. Because of the hazard in using these chemicals, always work in a well-ventilated area, use as

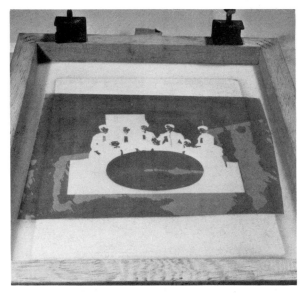

4.28 The light gray areas indicate poor adhesion.

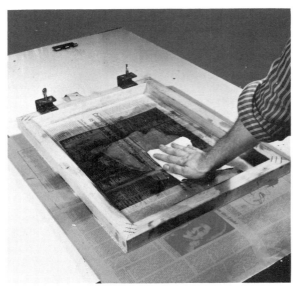

4.31 Scrubbing with pad of paper toweling to dissolve stencil.

Now lift the screen and peel off the newspaper that has stuck to it. Much of the stencil will come away with it (Figure 4.32). Repeat this process until the stencil is removed with perhaps only a few spots or a haze remaining.

Stand the screen up, and with two pads of toweling saturated with thinner, scrub both sides simultaneously, working only on

4.29 Sprinkling lacquer thinner (methyl alcohol) on pad of newspaper beneath screen.

4.30 Lacquer thinner (methyl alcohol) being sprinkled on lowered screen.

4.32 Peeling off layer of newspaper with much of the dissolved stencil.

a small area at a time. Refold or replace the pads as they become stained with stencil; resaturate them as they become dry. Continue working in this manner until all traces of the stencil are removed. If there are stubborn areas, use acetone or ethylene dichloride on them. Usually, a ghost of the image remains, but this results from ink pigment stain, rather than from the stencil.

PROBLEMS AND SOLUTIONS

Up to now we have assumed that everything has worked perfectly, but this is frequently not the case. Even the most practiced hand may encounter unexpected difficulties or cause something to go wrong. What follows are the more common problems, their solutions and preventions.

1. Too much pressure was applied in cutting the stencil.

This is the most common problem. Rather than discarding a stencil because of a few mistakes, an alteration in the adhering procedure is employed. Preparing a stencil requires cutting the edges of shapes, and adhering is concerned with maintaining those edges. What happens in broad nonprinting areas of the stencil can always be corrected with block-out without affecting the printing areas.

If there is only minor creasing in a few places, follow the adhering procedure described above, taking care to quickly dry up those areas where the creasing occurs.

If there is a great deal of creasing, the use of generous quantities of adhering fluid should be avoided, since it will pool up in the creases and melt the stencil edges. Proceed with the first application of adhering fluid as described above, but work more quickly and do not use as much fluid. Pay particular attention to areas of creasing and of fine detail. As you are working over the stencil, keep track of the problem areas to see whether or not they subsequently lighten up. If they do, they have become detached again.

Instead of repeating the application of adhering fluid in the same way, use a pad only lightly dampened with the fluid and press it gently onto the unadhered areas, remove and press with a finger (Figure 4.33). Working in this manner, try to adhere a sufficient portion of the shape or detail to permit the later removal of the backing sheet without tearing or deforming the unadhered portions. When you have

adhered as much of the stencil as possible, allow it to dry for about half an hour so that the unadhered portions will not stretch when the backing sheet is removed.

4.33   Pressing finger onto unadhered or poorly adhered area.

The backing sheet should be removed with even more care than before, especially as you come to those areas where shapes or details are barely attached to the screen. As a rule, the backing sheet should be pulled off at right or oblique angles to the edges of shapes. Where edges are not adhered at all, it is better to pull the backing sheet off parallel to the edge, but from behind. If it is difficult to remove the backing sheet, separate the stencil from the sheet with a fingernail or a dull palette knife.

Once the backing sheet is removed, replace it on the pack-up, lower the screen, and go over the entire stencil with a pad lightly dampened with adhering fluid, following quickly with a dry pad. With the creased backing sheet detached, the previously unadhered stencil edges quickly and easily become adhered with a minimum of fluid.

2. A piece of stencil accidentally peels off during cutting.

This is not an uncommon problem when working with small detail, very complicated stencils, or several stencils layered together during cutting.

If the piece has been only partially peeled off, it can be left in place and adhered along with the rest of the stencil. If it has been removed completely, it should be adhered separately after the rest of the stencil has been adhered and the backing sheet removed.

To do so, lay the backing sheet on the pack-up and position the stray piece. Lower the screen. Using a damp pad, go over the piece quickly and follow immediately with a dry pad. The piece may wrinkle a bit, but this will cause no problems in printing.

If the piece is fairly large, say, greater than 2 inches square, it is advisable to recut the loose piece on a small piece of stencil. This also applies if a piece is peeled off and lost. The problem with large unattached pieces is that they tend to deform and wrinkle to such an extent that registration problems or poor adhesion result. When adhering a recut piece, follow the general procedure for stencil adhesion, but try to avoid going over the previously adhered areas.

3. An edge or small shape dissolves during adhesion.

This is a common problem with badly creased stencils or where too much adhering fluid is used. Sometimes careful painting in with a clear lacquer or another block-out material will restore the area sufficiently (Figures 4.34 and 4.35).

However, where a sharp, clean edge is essential, recutting a piece of stencil to conform to the missing edge or shape is necessary. Allow for overlap into the remaining portion of the stencil. Position the piece under the screen. Using a lightly dampened pad, press onto the new piece. Remove the pad and press with a finger. When you are certain that it is adhered and dry, lift the screen and gently lift an edge of the new piece that overlaps the previously adhered stencil. With a brush apply some adhering fluid onto the overlapping surfaces (Figure 4.36). Lower the screen and press down where the two areas overlap. When dry, peel the backing sheet off the new piece of stencil. If some

4.34　Upper right corner shows the printed effect of a dissolved edge of a lacquer stencil.

4.35　Upper right corner shows the effect of a painted correction.

of the new patch is still loose, paint it with adhering fluid.

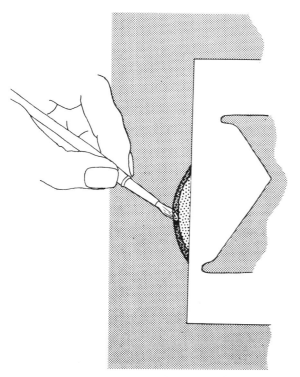

4.36 Brushing adhering fluid on the overlap of the patch and original stencil.

4. A small scrap of stencil has become adhered in a printing area.

When you are doing fine detail, with lots of small stencil scraps floating around, it is easy to overlook one, only to discover it later adhered where it is not wanted. If it is in the center of a printing area, it can be easily removed by pressing it between two pads dampened with adhering fluid for a few moments. The remaining residue can be scrubbed off with the pads.

Occasionally, small scraps can be gently pried loose with a fingernail or a dull palette knife or by poking with a needle or pin from the inside (Figure 4.37). These methods should be used to remove scrap that overlaps into a needed shape. If the scrap does not come off, it will have to be soaked off by pressing it between two pads dampened with adhering fluid (as described above). A repair will then have to be made for those areas that have been damaged in the process.

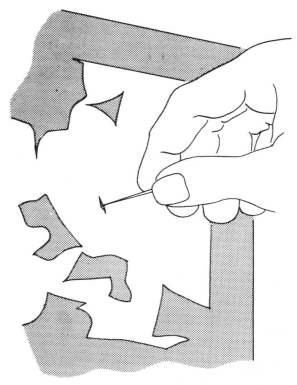

4.37 Using a pin (from inside of screen) to dislodge an unwanted scrap of stencil.

5. Portions of the stencil come off when the backing sheet is removed.

This is usually the result of insufficient adhering fluid or an improperly cleaned screen. If the backing sheet has not been entirely removed, lower the screen and readhere the stencil, exercising care in those areas that are detached. If it remains difficult to get good adhesion, press firmly on the stencil with the dampened pad to get sufficient adhesion to remove the backing sheet without deforming the stencil. Readhere where necessary after the backing sheet is removed. Under such conditions the screen may be insufficiently clean to begin with, or the adhering fluid incompatible with the stencil. Thoroughly clean the screen with acetone in the future, and check to determine that the adhering fluid makes the stencil tacky, not slippery.

SPECIAL EFFECTS

During the removal of a stencil you may discover certain effects that might be desirable in a print. If the stencil is only barely adhered to a screen, peeling and

4.38   Effect produced by tearing lacquer stencil (at left and bottom).

4.39   Selective melting of a lacquer stencil. A layer of paper toweling saturated in lacquer thinner was placed beneath the screen and the stencil rubbed from inside with a dampened pad. When the toweling was peeled away some of the lacquer stencil came with it.

tearing portions of it may create interesting edges and shapes (Figure 4.38). And placing a heavily textured material beneath the screen and then blotting it with a pad soaked in lacquer thinner, will create textures in the lacquer stencil (Figure 4.39).

If a stencil was left on the screen for a long time, line-drawing effects may emerge when the stencil is removed. When the newspaper is peeled away after the first application of lacquer thinner, most of the stencil will come away, leaving an outline along the edges of the shapes. The resulting print will be a white line on a dark field.

WATER-SOLUBLE STENCILS

Only a few water-soluble knife-cut stencils are available. They are intended to have the same cutting and stripping properties as lacquer stencils, but, in fact, they vary more than do lacquer films. The principal

advantages are that they do not require the use of highly volatile solvents and can be printed with lacquer and plastic inks.

Although all such films are water-soluble, plain water is seldom used because of their slowness in adhering and drying.

Usually a solution of isopropyl alcohol and water or acetic acid is used. Acetic acid in the form of white vinegar aids in softening the film, causing it to adhere rapidly to the fabric. The isopropyl alcohol increases the penetration of the film and accelerates the drying of the stencil.

ULANO'S AQUA FILM

Ulano's Aqua Film is one of the best water-soluble films and is the most similar to the better lacquer stencils in its cutting, stripping, and adhering features. It cuts easily and smoothly, strips away cleanly, and adheres rapidly with no distortion or deformation.

It can be used with any type of block-out material, although commercial water-soluble types are preferable because they dry rapidly without affecting the stencil and can be removed along with the stencil.

Unlike most lacquer stencils, which require a multifilament screen fabric, this stencil can be used on nylon, polyester, and wire.

STENCIL CUTTING

In cutting water-soluble film, the knife should be as sharp as possible since the film is somewhat tougher than most lacquer films. It is important to prevent the knife from leaning to one side during cutting as this film has a tendency to lift off the backing sheet along cut edges.

There is a tendency to use too much pressure in cutting this film because it is difficult to see the cuts and because the film feels like it is resisting the knife when it is not.

If a piece becomes stripped off accidentally, readhere it to the backing sheet with rubber cement immediately or it will curl up. Rubber cement is unaffected by the adhering fluid.

If, during cutting, edges tend to curl and lift off, it either means that your knife is too dull, you are leaning it to one side, or the film has dried out. This film should be kept in its original tube until needed, and not be left out when not in use. Film that has been left out for prolonged periods loses moisture and will delaminate from the backing sheet. The film can be re-moistened (before it lifts off) by keeping a damp sponge in the tube but not in contact with the film.

The stencils should not be cut far in advance of being used; however, once the stencil is adhered to the screen it can be left there indefinitely.

ADHERING

As with lacquer types, this stencil is taped in position to the underside of the screen with the cut side in contact with the fabric. The appropriate pack-up is placed beneath the screen.

The manufacturer recommends as adhering fluids either a mixture of three parts water to one part of 99 percent isopropyl alcohol or one part of 99 percent isopropyl alcohol to two parts of white vinegar.

I find that the alcohol/vinegar mixture works best. If a stronger, faster-working fluid is desired, the amount of vinegar can be increased.

Some drugstores carry 99 percent isopropyl alcohol, but 70 percent is much

4.40   Example of a print in which water-soluble knife-cut stencils were used.

more common. In my experience 70 percent alcohol works just as well, except that drying time is lengthened.

When applying the adhering fluid, use a cloth that is reasonably lint-free. Do not use paper toweling because the water in the adhering fluid causes it to come apart and leave particles of paper fibers embedded in the printing areas of the screen.

Completely saturate the cloth with the fluid and soak an area of about 10 inches square (Figure 4.41). Immediately follow with a dry cloth to remove excess fluid (Figure 4.42). In both application and drying, use as little pressure as possible. Since the film swells considerably and becomes quite gummy, the slightest pressure in rubbing can deform or melt the edges of shapes.

If creases in the backing sheet cause poor contact, very carefully press down in those areas with a finger. If some areas are impossible to adhere before removing the backing sheet, make sure that the stencil is thoroughly dry before removing the backing sheet and readhere those areas immediately after its removal. If you fail to do it promptly, the edges will curl away from the screen and become impossible to adhere.

If edges become melted, paint them in with a water-soluble block-out rather than attempting a patch because of the sus-

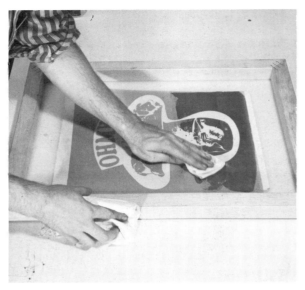

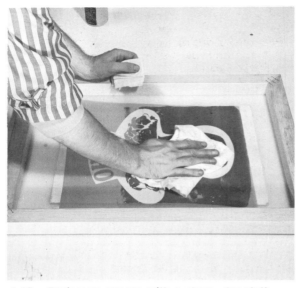

4.41 Application of adhering fluid with a saturated cloth.

4.42 Drying up excess with a clean, dry cloth.

ceptibility of the stencil to the adhering fluid.

Unwanted spots or pieces of stencil can be removed simply by using straight vinegar.

REMOVING THE STENCIL

One other advantage of water-soluble stencils is that it is possible to remove the stencil without washing it out. By working at a corner with a moistened finger, it is usually possible to detach enough of the stencil to permit it to be grasped and stripped off the screen completely (Figure 4.43). Any residue can then be washed off with two pads of paper toweling soaked in vinegar. If this does not work, the stencil will dissolve away cleanly in a warm water spray.

CRAFTINT WATER-SOLUBLE STENCIL

Craftint is quite different from Aqua Film. It is a gelatin-impregnated fibrous material. It cuts more like paper than like a lacquer stencil. Adhesion can be accomplished with an alcohol/water or alcohol/vinegar mixture or water, but it never adheres as tightly as Aqua Film.

Because it is fibrous, it requires a very

sharp knife and more pressure in cutting. It prints cleanly for moderate-size detail, but because it is thicker than Aqua Film and lacquer stencils, fine detail tends to plug up during printing.

Although it is not susceptible to deformation during adhesion, too much rubbing can wash out the gelatin, leaving only the unadhered fibrous material.

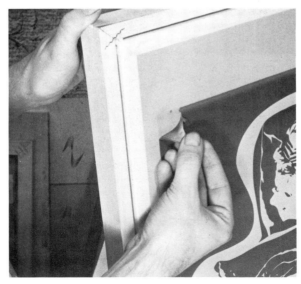

4.43 Peeling the stencil from the screen.

Like the Aqua Film, it can be easily stripped off the screen when printing is finished. Unfortunately, it sometimes strips off during printing or storage as well.

This film must be used on a multi-filament fabric.

REGISTRATION OF PRINTING PAPER

Any time you plan to print more than one color it is advisable to set up registration tabs for the printing paper before you adhere your first stencil. Not only are you able to easily position the first stencil where you want it on the paper, but all subsequent stencils can be easily registered to the previously printed colors.

The tabs should be permanent enough, at best, to survive an entire printing of all colors, and, at least, to hold up for the complete printing of one color.

Commercially there are several types of permanent tabs or stops employed, but for most purposes a simple tab made from kraft gummed tape will be excellent.

Select and cut your printing paper to the size you want. Position the paper in the center beneath your screen. With a pencil draw a line along the bottom and along one side of the paper on the printing surface (Figure 4.44).

Cut three pieces of gummed tape, 2" x 3". Fold the tape so that the back edge of the inside fold is visible, as shown in Figure 4.45. Wet the tape and position it with the back edge of the inside fold along the drawn line. Two pieces are placed on the side and one on the bottom, as shown.

4.45 Placement of kraft tape registration tabs showing their size and shape and how folded.

Rub these down hard with your fingers to make sure they are well seated, especially on nonporous surfaces. These should hold up very well, provided that water does not come in contact with them.

If they should start to peel up or lift off during printing, they can be temporarily held in place with masking tape. Masking tape cannot be used as a permanent tab since the cement is soluble in all of the solvents used in adhesion, printing, and clean-up.

If it becomes necessary to replace a tab, do it between color printings so as not to affect the registration during printing.

Kraft gummed tape tabs will not work in all situations. If cardboard or Masonite or other thick stocks are being printed, allowance must be made for the thickness of the material. The tab must be strong enough to withstand the abuse of the heavier material. A simple solution is to use tabs made from the printing stock or any material of the same thickness. These can be taped in place, for lighter-weight

4.44 Drawing pencil lines on printing surface to indicate placement of registration tabs.

stocks, or cemented down with hide glue or contact cement, for heavier stocks (Figure 4.46). If the material being printed is thick but flimsy and tends to ride over the stop, then a flap can be taped on top of the tab to prevent its doing so.

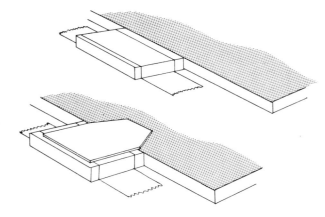

4.46   Registration tabs used for printing on thick materials.

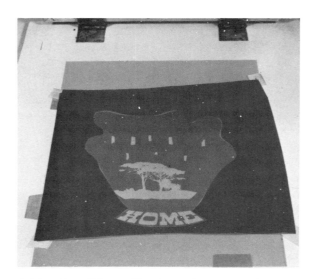

4.47   Stencil in position beneath screen with tape face up at corners.

POSITIONING THE STENCIL ON THE SCREEN

When you are printing more than one color, or when the position of the print on the paper is important, the stencil must be registered and temporarily attached to the screen before adhering.

To do this, place the screen in its hinges and place a piece of printing paper in the registration tabs. Place the stencil on the printing paper so that the printed image will be where you want it. Place a piece of masking tape, sticky side up, on each corner of the stencil, with each piece extending about one inch (Figure 4.47).

Lower the screen, and gently press down in the center with one hand, and with the other hand rub from the center out to each corner to ensure that the tape sticks securely.

Lift the screen carefully and check to see if the stencil is lying reasonably flat on the screen. If loose, lift the tape off each corner in turn and gently stretch out the stencil, corner by corner.

STENCIL BLOCK-OUT

There are several methods and materials for blocking out the unwanted portions of the screen opening. The types chosen are usually determined by the nature of the stencil and ink used. Whenever possible, use a block-out that is compatible with the stencil and that can be removed with the same solvent.

The most commonly used block-out materials are tapes, paper, hide glue, lacquers, and commercial water-soluble block-outs.

MASKING TAPE

Because of its thickness, which prevents good contact between the screen fabric and the printing paper, resulting in poor passage of ink, masking tape is usually used outside the printing area. Masking tape is frequently used at the top and bottom of the screen to tape paper block-outs in position. These are always placed on the under (printing) side of the screen. Occasionally masking tape is used at the top and bottom as the block-out material itself. In this case it is placed on the squeegee side of the screen.

Emergencies such as pinholes in non-printing areas may develop during printing. Masking tape is frequently used on the underside of the screen to cover these holes.

A principal disadvantage of masking tape is that the cement is soluble in all the solvents used in silkscreen, becoming gummy and shifting or lifting off.

Masking tape must be removed prior to cleaning ink from the screen.

CELLOPHANE TAPE

The advantage of cellophane tape is that it is considerably thinner than masking tape. When it is necessary to use tape close to printing areas it is better to use cellophane tape. The cement on cellophane tape is also susceptible to all solvents, and must be removed from the screen prior to ink clean-up.

PAPER

Paper is commonly used as a temporary mask or block-out for short printing runs at the top and bottom of the screen if there is considerable space between the edge of the stencil and the outside of the screen opening (Figure 4.48).

4.48 **Use of paper and masking tape to block out unwanted areas of the screen.**

Any reasonably thin, nonporous paper will do. Always seal all edges over which the squeegee will pass with strips of masking tape. This prevents the paper from shifting and the ink from bleeding underneath onto the printing surface.

Paper block-outs are always placed on the under (printing) side of the screen and should be removed prior to ink clean-up.

LACQUER BLOCK-OUT

A lacquer block-out is commonly used with lacquer stencils. Both are soluble in lacquer thinner, and thus the stencil and block-out are removed at the same time.

Prepared block-outs are available, but any clear lacquer can be used. Generally, ordinary lacquers are diluted 25 percent with lacquer thinner.

The cheapest, most expedient lacquer block-out is made from scraps of stripped lacquer stencil dissolved in thinner. The solution should have the consistency of heavy cream.

COMMERCIAL WATER-SOLUBLE BLOCK-OUTS

Several types of water-soluble block-out are found in the market. Their principal advantage is that they are not affected by most inks and can be washed out with cold water. They apply easily and dry rapidly because of their very volatile solvents.

It is recommended that they be used with water-soluble stencils (photographic, knife-cut) and not with lacquer types. The solvent in the block-out readily combines with lacquer stencils and creates a mixture that can only be removed with the block-out's particular solvent.

Another caution is to be observed: be absolutely sure that the block-out is thoroughly dry before printing or allowing any other solvent to come in contact with it. If the tacky block-out comes in contact with wet ink or turpentine, it also becomes insoluble in anything except its own solvent.

Screens that have a heavy shellac on the mask should not be used with commercial water-soluble block-outs for the same reasons.

Because many of these block-outs contain highly volatile solvents, such as ethylene dichloride or methyl chloride, they should be kept tightly closed when not in use and should be used only in well-ventilated areas. The same instructions apply when you are using these solvents to remove stubborn spots of block-out from a screen.

If block-outs become thickened with age, the appropriate thinner should be used. Usually this is either two parts of ethylene dichloride and one part methyl (wood) alcohol, or two parts methyl chloride and one part ethyl alcohol. By experimenting with some types you will find that the alcohol component alone is sufficient for thinning.

When reclaiming a screen, the water-soluble block-out should always be removed before the stencil. Most manufacturers advise using only cold water, as hot water causes the formation of an insoluble substance. When washing out, the screen is free of block-out when it no longer feels slippery.

HIDE GLUE BLOCK-OUT

Any of the hide glues generally available at hardware stores can be used as block-outs. Their consistency as purchased is too thick and requires thinning with an equal amount of water. If not thinned, the block-out may develop cracks, which may print if you are printing with very thin inks.

If the glue is old or cloudy, it may be advisable to mix two parts of glue to one part of water. Hide glue does spoil, especially when exposed to air or stored in metal cans. It develops a very strong, sour smell and becomes extremely cloudy. If this is the case, discard it. Mix the glue for block-out as needed, rather than mixing and storing it in large volumes.

Hide glue withstands most solvents well, except for prolonged scrubbing with acetone or lacquer thinners, which may cause pinholes to develop. It washes out easily with water at any temperature.

If you use this block-out with a gelatin photo stencil, it is particularly important to remove all traces of it prior to removing the photo stencil, as the enzyme used to remove the stencil will render the block-out totally insoluble.

AQUA FILM BLOCK-OUT

If you are using Ulano's Aqua Film, save the stripped scraps and dissolve them in water, vinegar and water, or water and alcohol. (The percentages are not important.) The advantage of this block-out is its compatibility with water-soluble stencils and its immediate availability.

APPLYING A LIQUID BLOCK-OUT

To apply any liquid block-out, paint it on directly with a brush, or spread it on with a small squeegee or a piece of cardboard. In small areas within the printing area, or along edges where the stencil meets the screen mask, brushing is easiest.

For large areas it is best to spread it on. Elevate the screen so that it does not touch the printing surface. Use a piece of

cardboard about 2 inches by 3 inches. Pour a puddle into the well, but not on the fabric, or it may drip through. In a snow-plow fashion, spread the material back and forth until the area is covered (Figure 4.49). Work out all drips and beads. Allow to dry and inspect for pinholes. If there are any, repeat the application.

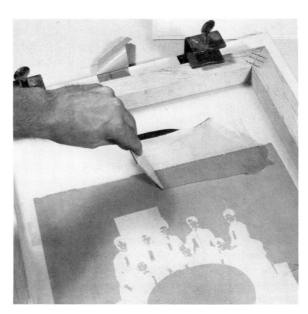

4.49 Spreading the liquid block-out over the open areas with a small piece of cardboard.

COLOR REGISTRATION

The following discussion of registration situations that arise in multicolor printing is presented here instead of in the chapter on printing because when preparing stencils, certain decisions must be made regarding the sequence in which the various colors will be printed.

DARK COLOR SHAPE AGAINST LIGHT COLOR FIELD

This is the easiest of all multicolor situations. Whether or not this sequence is followed depends entirely on the hiding power of the second color, since it will be printed over the first. As a common-sense rule, white has the least hiding power—and black has the greatest. Colors tend to show through white, and black covers other colors completely even when thinned considerably.

Consider a printing situation in which a

blue circle appears on a yellow rectangle. A separate stencil is needed for each color. Since the yellow is the lighter color, it will be printed first. Since blue will sufficiently cover or hide yellow, the yellow can be printed as a solid field, and the stencil for the yellow will be a rectangular hole in the stencil material.

4.50   A two-color overprint. The dark color, blue, is printed over the light color, yellow.

After the yellow stencil is prepared, another piece of stencil material is taped over it and the blue circle is cut precisely and stripped away. With a pen, mark the four corners of the yellow ground color on the blue stencil. This permits accurate placement of the second stencil after the first is printed.

The yellow stencil is then attached to the screen, printed and removed.

When the yellow print is dry, place a copy in the registration tabs as for printing. Position the blue stencil on the print, using the pen marks as a guide. Place tape on each of the four corners, sticky side up with about an inch extending. Gently lower the screen and attach the stencil to it. The blue stencil is now in register to the first color. After adhesion and block-out you are ready to print.

Be sure to print the first color with the printing paper carefully positioned in the registration tabs. Carelessness or absence of tabs will make it impossible to maintain registration of the blue stencil.

It is likewise important not to remove the screen from the hinges if clamp hinges are used, and to make sure that there is as little play in the screen hinges as possible.

LIGHT COLOR SHAPE AGAINST DARK COLOR FIELD

This is the most difficult of stencil situations. In the previously described situation slight shifts in registration will not have a noticeable effect. But here any inaccuracy in stencil preparation, adhesion, or printing can produce an unwanted white line between shapes (Figure 4.51).

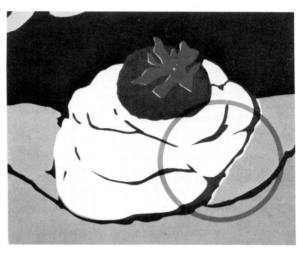

4.51   Insufficient overlap in stencil preparation produces white lines in the print.

The following procedure is used whenever it is not possible to overprint because of poor hiding power of the second color or when the resulting build-up from successive printing is undesirable.

Inverting the example to now use a yellow circle against a blue rectangle, the yellow will again be printed first, but the blue, now the ground color, will **not** be printed as a solid field.

The stencil for the yellow is prepared by cutting a hole corresponding to the shape of the yellow area, but slightly larger wherever it will be in contact with the blue.

Since in any printing situation perfect registration is impossible, allowance must be made for slight variations in stencil preparation and printing technique. To compensate for this, wherever two colors butt up against each other, overlap must be provided in cutting the stencil for the

4.52 Two colors printed in butt registration. The dark color, brown, is printed over the light color, blue.

first printed color. The second (or successive) color(s) will then define the final shape of the lighter colors previously printed (Figure 4.52).

How much overlap to provide depends on such variables as the rigidity of screen hinges, the tautness of the fabric, the accuracy of stencil cutting and adhesion, and the care taken in positioning the paper. Only experience can teach you what will work best in different situations.

As a rule, $\frac{1}{16}$- to $\frac{1}{8}$-inch overlap is sufficient. Smaller screens generally require less overlap than do large ones.

The blue stencil will be a rectangular hole with a piece of stencil in the same place and exactly the shape planned for the yellow circle. After the yellow is dry, the blue stencil is positioned over it so that yellow clearly shows around the edge

of the center shape on the blue stencil. The second color is then printed, overlapping the first color and thus preventing an unwanted white line between the shapes.

TRANSPARENT LIGHT COLOR AGAINST DARK COLOR FIELD
To get a green circle on a blue rectangle by printing blue and yellow, two methods may be used. In the first, a blue opaque field is printed solidly, and the precise yellow circle is printed very transparently over it, producing the green. In the second, the precise yellow circle is printed opaquely first, and then a solid field of transparent blue is printed over it to produce the green.

The stencils are the same in either case. The blue is a rectangular hole, the

yellow is the circle. As a rule, however, it is always preferable to print light colors over dark ones where transparent effects are desired because of the inherent transparency of lighter colors. Also, when dark colors are made extremely transparent and printed on white paper, they tend to look weaker and lighter than desired.

TRANSPARENT DARK COLOR AGAINST LIGHT COLOR FIELD

The stencils are prepared as above, except the rectangular stencil is the yellow and the circle shape is the blue. Either color may be printed first, as long as the second color is sufficiently transparent.

5. photo stencil tec

nniques: the positive

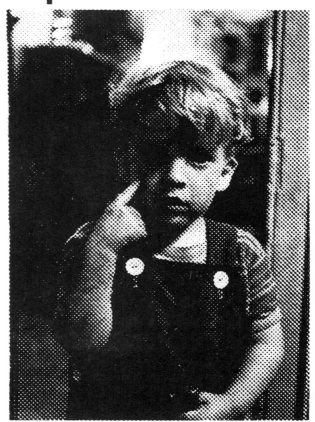

In recent years there has been a rise in popular interest in photo stencil techniques, although these techniques have been known and used by commercial processors for over fifty years. Photo stencil processes take their name from the fact that the materials used are sensitive to light. They are not photographic in the conventional sense—that is, they do not take or make finished pictures.

Many people believe that a great, new world of graphic effects will open to them if they turn to photo stencil techniques, but the effects achieved derive from the creativity and ingenuity of the artist and are not inherent in the process. The quality and nature of the photo stencil relates directly to the quality and nature of the positive used to control the exposure. The process merely permits the achievement of certain effects that are unobtainable with other stencil techniques, but that are for the most part known to anyone who does a great deal of drawing, painting, or photography.

The mention of photographic silkscreen also conjures up, in the minds of many, notions of complicated and expensive tools, materials, and techniques. The truth, however, is that anyone who is already doing silkscreen printing will have no trouble acquiring the necessary techniques and will find it not much more expensive than any of the other processes.

Those who are interested in making photo stencils must understand what happens in their preparation. The materials of the stencils are highly sensitive to ultraviolet light. They are called light-hardening emulsions because they can be made insoluble in water upon exposure. Where ultraviolet light is blocked from the emulsion, the emulsion will wash away, and ink will pass through the screen.

Ways to block the ultraviolet light from the stencil during exposure is the subject of this chapter. That is, we are concerned here with the making of a "positive"—positive because it looks exactly like the printed image—that will be used to block the light. (The terms "reverse negative," "positive transparency," and "film positive" are also used.) In any positive, the areas that are to print must block the ultraviolet light completely, and those that are **not** to print must pass light freely.

There are two ways to put an idea into a positive form suitable for use in making a photo stencil: (1) photographically—by means of film positives, electrostatic transparencies, photostatic transparencies, and so on; and (2) mechanically—by means of hand drawings, photomechanical aids, lift transfers, and so on.

Commercially, all positives are made photographically. The original art or drawing is prepared in black and white on illustration board and photographed onto sheet film, which may then be enlarged or reduced or repeated as needed. If one works with photographic images or pictures, the photographic positive is about the only way to achieve a faithful result.

Handmade (mechanical) positives do not entail the expense of having film positives made by others. And the artist does not have to possess special skills or elaborate equipment. All the effects obtainable with drawing can be obtained in this way. The principal disadvantage of handmade positives is their inability to reproduce original photographic images.

FILM POSITIVES FOR MONOCHROME IMAGES

Presenting complete details for producing photographic film positives is beyond the scope of this book. Anyone who has undertaken to enlarge and print his own film will find it easy to make film positives. Those who have not, and who are not generally familiar with darkroom procedure, should obtain a simple basic book on black-and-white photography.

Many, many brands of film are available for use in making positives. Practically all are of the orthochromatic type—they are insensitive to red light. This "red blindness" is particularly well suited to the making of positives, since such film is by nature contrasty. As a result, an ortho film positive will be transparently clear and opaquely black.

Commercially, special process cameras are used to make a full-size negative from the original artwork. This is contact-printed to another sheet of film to produce the positive.

To make a film positive with an enlarger, a contrasty negative, obtained with an ordinary camera, is projected onto a sheet of ortho film, and test strips are made to determine the proper exposure for the positive. Select the strip in which solid, opaque blacks first appear.

If the desired degree of contrast is not

obtained, the film can be reduced to remove unwanted grays and then intensified to make the blacks opaque. Generally, as long as the blacks are opaque, a slight veil in the clear areas will not adversely affect the stencil.

Any unwanted clear areas in the positive can be opaqued out with photo opaque applied to the emulsion side of the film. Similarly, unwanted opaque areas can be removed by selectively applying a bleaching agent (such as Farmer's reducer) or by scraping away the emulsion with a sharp stencil knife or a lithographer's needle.

Another method of achieving the necessary contrast in the positive without reducing and intensifying requires contact-printing back and forth on successive sheets of film until all unwanted grays are removed and all blacks are opaque. The first projection-printed positive is contact-printed to a second sheet of film. After processing, this is contact-printed to a third sheet of film. This process is continued until a suitable positive is achieved. Some people prefer this approach because it permits them to determine through exposure control which grays will disappear and which will become black.

LINE-DRAWING EFFECTS

Line-drawing effects can be achieved, simply and directly, in four basic steps.

A suitable negative is projection-printed onto a sheet of ortho film. After processing, it is reduced and intensified (if necessary) to remove unwanted grays and increase opacity of the blacks.

This film positive is then contact-printed, emulsion side to emulsion side, to another sheet of ortho film, producing a same-size film negative. Avoid reducing and intensifying this, since it can alter the distribution of lights and darks, making it impossible to register it to the positive.

The two sheets of film are then placed in perfect register to one another, with their bases, not their emulsions, in contact. If registration is perfect, no light will be visible through them.

A third sheet is placed beneath this sandwich. Exposure now differs from ordinary contact-printing, for the perfectly registered positive and negative films can pass no light at right angles. But there is sufficient space for the light to pass through at an angle, since the bases of the positive and negative are in contact.

Achieving the line effect is now easy.

Raise the enlarger head to the top and set the lens at an intermediate aperture. Set your timer for about ten seconds (the actual time must be determined by test). Hold the contact printing frame at a 45-degree angle in the center of the cone of light and expose the film (Figure 5.1). Turn the frame and repeat the exposure for all four sides, and then process the film. If a white line on a dark field is desired, this film can be used to make a photo stencil. If the reverse is wanted, contact-print this film to a fourth sheet of film, which then is used to produce the final photo stencil.

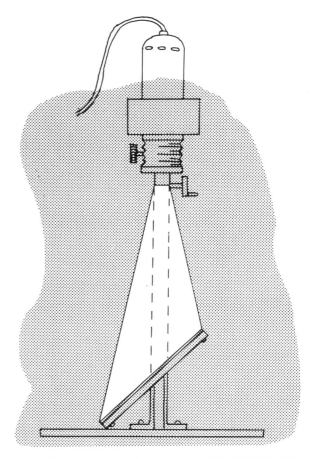

5.1 Exposure arrangement used for making line-drawing effect positives.

Where more texture is desired in the image, you can experiment with continuous tone negatives or positives for the sandwich. The results can be exciting and surprising.

PAPER POSITIVES

Under some circumstances photographic printing paper can be used to make a positive. A single weight #6 or ortho printing paper should provide the necessary contrast and allow sufficient translucency. If necessary to increase transparency, you can coat the back of the paper with Vaseline or mineral oil. The prints must be thoroughly washed to remove all traces of chemicals. The disadvantages are that photographic printing paper greatly increases the exposure time needed to prepare the photo stencil and causes a loss of fine detail in the stencil.

HALFTONE POSITIVES

The positives previously described are called "line positives." They have translated all the grays of the original photography into areas of black and white with little or no illusion of gray in the final positives. Not all subjects lend themselves to this treatment, and for some people the effect is not photographic enough.

To preserve the appearance of the original in the positive, the grays must be converted into dots of opaque black surrounded by transparent white because the stencil materials exist only in a print or no-print state. By varying the size of the dots, the illusion of the various grays is created. When the dots are very large, the grays appear dark; where they are small they appear light. The resulting positive is called a "screened" or "halftone positive" (Figure 5.2).

Commercially, a one-color image is screened when the original negative is made. When you are projection-printing film positives, a contact screen may be placed in tight contact over the sheet of film in the easel. The resulting positive will have the grays represented in variously sized dots.

Although the most common screen creates circular dots, there are contact screens that create line patterns, fabric textures, concentric circles, square dots, and so on. All are quite expensive, start-

5.2　Comparison of a line print and a halftone print. The halftone was made with a 30-line screen and printed 3 inches by 4½ inches.

ing at about $20 for an 8" x 10" screen. However, many other interesting textures and patterns are available in rub-down and dry-transfer photomechanical materials (Zip-a-Tone, Paratone, etc.), and they can be used fairly effectively as contact screens. Their disadvantage is that they are particularly coarse, creating large and noticeable dots or patterns.

Because the halftone stencil is itself carried on a woven fabric, certain limitations are encountered when choosing the kind and fineness of screen fabric to use. Halftone screens generally range from 45 to 300 lines (dots) per linear inch. Since usually one wants the smallest dot possible, this means using the finest screen mesh possible. As a rule—to ensure that even the smallest dots will have enough threads to hold them in place—the ratio of fabric screen mesh to halftone screen line should be a minimum of 3 to 1. A 50-line halftone positive should then be printed on a screen with a mesh equivalent to 16xx or 155 threads per inch.

5.3   Moiré pattern resulting from improper positioning of halftone on screen.

A problem with halftone stencils is the creation of moiré patterns when the stencil is in certain positions on the screen (Figure 5.3). To avoid this, simply place the positive on a light table and rotate the screen slowly until the moiré patterns disappear. Then mark the screen to show where to position the stencil during adhesion.

SPECIAL FILMS

Two films are of particular interest to anyone wishing to make his own film positives. One is Kodak's Autopositive Film and the other is Kodak's Autoscreen Film 6563. The autopositive film permits the making of film positives or negatives directly from the original art without need of an enlarger, camera, or darkroom.

To make a positive with the Autopositive film from a black-and-white ink drawing, for example, place a sheet of film, emulsion-side down, on top of the drawing in a contact frame. Over this, place a sheet of yellow acetate. Exposure is made through the film with an arc lamp or #2 reflector photo floods. Develop the film with any of the Kodalith developers.

This film is particularly tolerant of room light. Low levels of tungsten or daylight fluorescent are permissible for up to nine minutes.

The film can also be used to make film positives from negatives by contact printing. Instead of exposing through the yellow acetate as above, the film is preflashed for two minutes with a yellow light. Then the normal contact-printing procedure is followed, using a white light.

Kodak's Autoscreen 6563 film has a halftone dot pattern incorporated in it, so that the resulting positive or negative is automatically screened. Since this film is designed principally to serve the offset lithographer, it has a 133-line screen, which is too fine for most silkscreen work, unless exceptionally fine meshes are used. The general practice is to enlarge the autoscreen positive or negative about 2 or 3 times to achieve a 40- to 65-line halftone.

Enlargement can be a drawback, however, if you do not have access to the necessary equipment. A way around this is to projection-print an original negative onto a sheet of autoscreen film, take another picture of the autoscreen positive, and finally projection-print this new negative onto conventional ortho film.

COMMERCIAL POSITIVES

With commercially made positives, as a rule, when you order a positive, you pay for a negative as well. Halftone positives are always more expensive than line positives. The prices for any one company are fixed, and within most metropolitan areas they are competitive.

You must give the processor camera-ready art: opaque blacks and clean whites. Photographs, when used, should be glossies. You also must indicate whether you wish a line or halftone positive, what line halftone you wish, such as a 50-line halftone, and the size of the final positive.

FILM POSITIVES FOR MULTICOLOR PHOTOGRAPHIC IMAGES

Many people will not be satisfied with simple monochrome line or halftone photographic images. Instead, color and photographic qualities are desired. Unfortunately, faithful reproduction of color is probably the most difficult task facing the professional photographer, screen processor, and printer. The experience, skill, knowledge of materials, techniques, equipment, and facilities are beyond the scope of this book.

However, if you are interested in creating exciting, multicolor photo images and in using color creatively in ways that are difficult to imagine and impossible to photograph, there are several techniques available to make the necessary positives. And none of the techniques is much more complicated than making line positives or one-color halftones.

COLOR FROM BLACK AND WHITE: POSTERIZATION

One of the easiest ways to get multicolor silkscreen prints from black-and-white photography is to plan for it when you are taking pictures. Using a high-contrast copy film in your camera and a tripod to hold the camera stationary, take a series of exposures of your subject—from vastly underexposed to vastly overexposed. Since these high-contrast films tend to render everything as opaquely black and clearly transparent, much as ortho films do, the underexposed negatives will record only bright highlights as black, and the over-

exposed ones will record everything as black except deep shadow.

A negative for each different color desired in the final silkscreen is projection-printed onto sheet ortho film to produce opaque blacks and clear, transparent whites. If you wish to have, say, three colors, select one negative that will print a normal-looking positive, one that shows highlight detail, and one that shows shadow detail. The positives are then used to make the necessary photo stencils (Figure 5.4).

5.4 Tone separation printed in three opaque colors, the lightest first. This particular separation was made with high-contrast copy film.

In printing the stencils from these positives, if a fairly naturalistic balance of light and dark is desired, the stencil from the darkest positive is printed first in the lightest color. The stencil from the lightest positive is printed last in the darkest color. This printing sequence is generally followed with opaque inks. With transparent inks or where deliberate color mixing is desired, the order of printing depends on the colors to be created.

If you are unable to use high-contrast copy film in your camera or already have a negative that you wish to separate into tones, this can be done also, but it is somewhat more complicated.

First, do test strips of your negative on a sheet of ortho film, setting your enlarger at minimum aperture and exposing at two-second intervals. Then select the strip in which shadow detail shows clearly and opaquely. If you want three positives for three colors, expose the first at the indicated exposure, the second at twice the first, and the third at twice the second. This will give you more or less equal intervals between all three and give you one positive that records mainly highlight detail, one that records mainly shadows, and one in between. If necessary, the positives may be reduced and intensified to remove grays and to increase the opacity of the blacks. These positives can then be used to make the photo stencils.

MULTICOLOR PRINTS FROM COLOR PHOTOGRAPHS

There are basically two different ways to render a color photograph or slide into the necessary separate black-and-white positives for photo stencil production. These are known as tone-line separations and halftone separations.

TONE-LINE SEPARATIONS

Tone-line separations are similar in appearance to black-and-white posterized prints. The process differs in that instead of varying the exposure to achieve the various positives, filters are used to separate the three colors inherent in color photos or slides. The filters most commonly used are: red-wratten #25, green-wratten #58, and blue-wratten #47B.

A high-contrast panchromatic film should be used because the film must be sensitive to the full spectrum. Since with this process you are basically printing broad flat areas of color, the film should be high-contrast to ensure maximum density of the blacks.

This process does not render photographs that are as realistic as halftones. However, if more faithful color balance is desired, a film like Super XX or Panatomic X can be used and processed as slightly dense continuous-tone negatives.

Since the films used in making the separation negatives are panchromatic, they must be handled in total darkness. The best way is in a camera. When working from slides, use a slide-copier attachment on your camera. When working from color photos, set your camera up on a tripod and set lights carefully for copy work. As a precaution, bracket your exposures so that you have several nega-

tives to choose from. The filters, mentioned above, are placed over the lens, and if you are using a hand-held light meter or exposure calculator, the filter factor must be taken into account when determining the exposure. After processing, the negatives that show dense blacks are projection-printed onto sheet ortho film to achieve the necessary positives for photo stencil production.

Where some semblance of naturalistic color is sought, the red-filtered positive will be printed in process blue (cyan), the green-filtered one will be printed in process red (magenta), and the blue-filtered one in process yellow. However, since these are tone separations, the degree of naturalism attained will depend mainly on the artist's ingenuity in color selection and sequence of color and stencil printing.

HALFTONE SEPARATIONS

Faithful halftone color separations and printing are the most difficult of all processes. Still, very dramatic and effective results can be obtained with the short method described below.

For halftone work you need a fine or moderate grain, medium-contrast panchromatic film. Super XX is still one of the standards, but for people with small cameras, Panatomic X will work fine.

Proceed as before to make the separation negatives. Since many people feel that the three colors alone lack dimensionality, a fourth separation is made that will be printed black. This separation is made by triple-exposing the film, once with each of the filters at the same exposures used for each of the color separations. If your camera does not allow for triple exposure, the three individual negative separations can be combined in the enlarger when you are printing the final halftone positive.

The separation negatives are projection-printed onto ortho film that has a halftone contact screen in tight contact on top. In order to prevent the formation of moiré patterns and to ensure that each dot will not be covered by the successive printing of the colors, the contact screen is rotated to a different position for each of the positives.

For three-color work, the red positive will have the contact screen 45 degrees off vertical. The green will have it 75 degrees clockwise off vertical, and the blue will be 105 degrees clockwise off vertical.

For four-color work, the black will be at 45 degrees off vertical, the green at 75 degrees, the blue at 90 degrees, and the red at 105 degrees.

After these halftone positives are processed, they may be selectively reduced or intensified in areas to strengthen or remove dots. However, the dots must have good opacity if they are to effectively hold back the light during photo stencil exposure.

For representational color printing, process colors are used: process red (magenta), process blue (cyan), process yellow, and process black. As mentioned before, the red-filtered positive will be printed in process blue, the green-filtered one in magenta, and the blue-filtered one in yellow.

The final effect of a silkscreen print made this way will have an obvious and direct relationship to a color photograph. But it will also be clearly different and uniquely a silkscreen rendering of a color photograph. The procedure for obtaining faithful full-color silkscreen reproductions is far too complicated to be covered here.

OTHER PROCESSES

Many people use photostatic positive transparencies. The quality of these is never as good as that of a film positive, but if the copy is reasonably high in contrast, it can be used effectively. Not all photostatic firms make transparencies, but their equipment is capable of making them.

Similarly, xerography or electrostatic processes are capable of making transparencies. Xerox does manufacture a plastic sheet that is suitable for some of their copiers and is not affected by the heat of the fusion chamber. The pigment in a Xerox copier is sufficiently opaque for photo stencil purposes.

The image obtained from a Xerox is altogether different from what one expects. Solid black shapes become outlined in black. The line-drawing quality is best when the artwork or photographs used are of high contrast with few intermediate grays.

Other ways to achieve a suitable positive for photo stencil work are beyond the reach of most people. But anyone with access to visual-aid production facilities should see what equipment is available for the making of transparencies for overhead projectors. Diazo, Ozalid, and 3M make such equipment, and in some cases the blacks are sufficiently opaque to be used as positives.

MECHANICAL OR HANDMADE POSITIVES

In handmade positives, the original art is prepared directly on a transparent or translucent material that permits light to pass through during exposure of the stencil. A number of materials can be used: clear and matte acetate, mylar, kronar, polyester, vinyl, tracing paper, vellum, and thin bond papers.

Probably the most versatile material is a matte acetate 3 to 5 mils thick. Matte acetate and any plastic are less likely to buckle than papers when using water-based drawing materials. The frosted surface of matte acetate has sufficient tooth to permit the use of inks and photo opaque without crawling. Dry materials such as conte, litho crayon, and graphite, which cannot be used on clear plastics, can also be used. Of all the plastics it is the cheapest. It is also considerably easier to see through than most papers. Corrections can be made easily by erasing or by scraping with a sharp stencil knife.

DRAWING MATERIALS
Any drawing material that can be put down opaquely can be used. Because the photo stencil emulsions are particularly sensitive to ultraviolet light, any material that blocks ultraviolet light can be used, even if it passes a portion of the visible spectrum.

Such materials as red photo opaque, opaque red lettering ink, and red acrylic paints need not be applied completely opaquely. However, when in doubt about a particular material, always apply it opaquely.

The following materials have been found to work well with a variety of stencil materials with different exposure systems (Figure 5.5):

1. India ink, applied with brush or pen.
2. Photo opaque, applied with brush or with pen.
3. Opaque red lettering inks, applied with brush or pen.
4. Red acrylic paints, applied with brush.

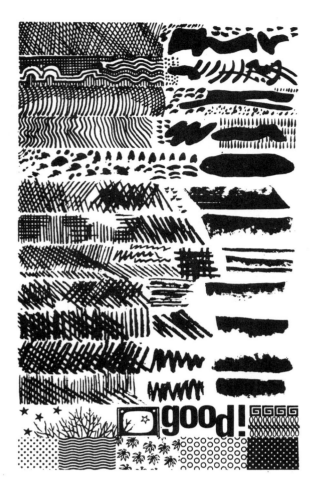

5.5 Examples of various materials used in making handmade positives. From top: India ink, photo opaque, opaque lettering ink (red), engrossing ink, red acrylic paint, conte crayon (sepia), lithographic crayon, ebony sketch pencil, stick graphite, compressed charcoal, oil pastels, pastels, dry-transfer photomechanical aids, rub-down photomechanical aids.

5. Engrossing inks, applied with brush or pen.

6. Sepia conte crayon, in stick or pencil.

7. Lithographic crayon, in stick or pencil.

8. China marker crayon.

9. Soft graphite, in stick or pencil.

10. Compressed charcoal, in stick or pencil.

11. Black or red oil pastels.

12. Dry-transfer materials.

13. Rub-down photomechanical aids.

Materials that do not work well include:

1. Felt tip and magic marker pens.

2. Fountain or rapidograph inks.

3. Water colors.

A wide variety of photomechanical aids used in commercial art can be used in making a positive. These include the dry-transfer and rub-down materials that are available in various type faces, textures, patterns, symbols, and so on. There are many brands such as Craftype, Craftint, Art Type, Art Tone, Zip-a-Tone, Paratone, Lettraset, Lettratone, Letterpress, and Microtype. One or more brands are usually carried by art or drafting supply stores. All such materials (in black) are sufficiently opaque.

With dry-transfer material the sheet containing the textures or symbols is positioned over the acetate. A blunt instrument, usually a burnisher, is used to rub over the area to be transferred, as the sheet is held firmly in place. Usually you can tell when the transfer is complete by the lighter appearance of the transferred material (Figure 5.7). Do not use a pencil or ballpoint pen, as these crease the sheet and cause the symbol or texture to deform or break apart.

When the material is transferred, the sheet is lifted off and the slip sheet is placed on top of the transfer and rubbed down hard (Figure 5.8). This ensures that the transfer is firmly adhered and decreases the possibility that it will be abraded off. A mistake can be easily removed by erasing it with a ball of dried rubber cement or the sticky side of a piece of masking tape or by scraping it off with a stencil knife. To increase the permanence of the transfer, spray it with a clear acrylic fixative.

Rub-down materials differ in that the sheet to which the symbols or textures are attached will also be attached to the positive.

The sheet of symbols is positioned on the positive and the image is rubbed down as before. A sharp stencil knife is used to cut out the shape and peel away the unwanted portion (Figure 5.9). These materials are best suited for broad areas of texture or patterns.

If you make a mistake, use the point of your stencil knife to lift a corner and peel the material away. Unlike dry-transfer materials, rub-down materials can be used again.

Both types of material have a waxlike adhesive that readily picks up dust and

5.6 A print made from a handmade positive. Photo opaque was used in pen and brush. Needles were used to produce white lines and cross-hatching.

5.7 Application of dry-transfer materials. Note that letter becomes lighter as it separates from the sheet and attaches to the surface below.

5.8 Rubbing over the transferred letter with the slip sheet in place to insure good adhesion.

5.9 Cutting away unwanted portions of rub-down material.

softens with the heat of your hand. Always work on a clean, dust-free surface, and keep the slip sheet between the symbol sheet and the work surface to prevent transferring from the heat and pressure of your hand.

LIGHT STAGES

When working on a positive, it is much easier to check the opacity of your drawing if you have a way of lighting it from behind.

A simple light stage for small positives can be made from a piece of ¼-inch frosted or translucent white Plexiglas, supported at an angle, with a high-intensity light positioned underneath (Figure 5.10).

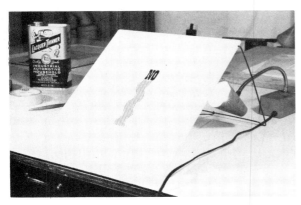

5.10 A simple light stage for working on positives.

For larger work a box can be built out of plywood with two or more 24-watt fluorescent fixtures inside and a ¼-inch translucent Plexiglas top.

If you are planning to do a great deal of photo stencil work, you may want to build a light table that can also be used as an exposure unit. See pp. 84–85 for information about such a unit.

When working with dry drawing materials that smudge, you may want to spray them with a clear acrylic or fixative during the work or after completing it. When spraying, tape your positive down securely to prevent curling. If you plan to do more work on it, use a matte or reworkable fixative. Do not saturate the acetate nor spray too close. Several light coatings are better than one heavy one. If the acetate takes on a pronounced curl, turn it over and spray the other side.

To keep the acetate flat, always store it flat, never rolled up.

LIFT TRANSFERS

There is a way to achieve "photographic" images without photography. The lift transfer, a cousin to collage, converts a printed photographic image from a magazine into a form suitable for use as a positive (Figure 5.11). The inks of most magazines are sufficiently opaque for use in a positive.

The trick is to separate the printed image from its paper. Only magazines printed on clay-coated papers—the so-called slicks—will work, since this clay (kaolin) is water-soluble and the ink rests on the clay, not on the paper.

Since the ink and clay layers are so thin—they disintegrate instantly in water—before any attempt is made to separate the ink from the paper, the ink has to be transferred to another surface. The transfer is usually done by building up several layers of acrylic polymer painting medium on top of the image before lifting it off the paper.

Although only two or three layers of the polymer medium are necessary to lift the ink, the resulting film is so thin that it is easily torn or deformed. It is best to build up six to eight layers of emulsion, if possible, before lifting. For added durability the lifted image can be laminated to a piece of clear or matte acetate.

The step-by-step procedure for making a lift-transfer positive follows.

5.11   A print from a photo stencil made from a lift-transfer positive.

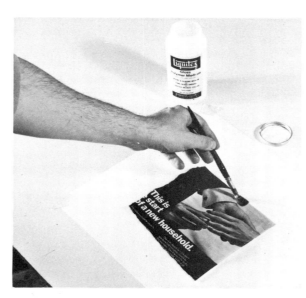

5.12   Brushing acrylic painting medium onto a magazine image that is to be lift-transferred.

1.   Select an image with reasonable contrast. Color images may be used, but there are no real rules to determine which color conditions work best. In general, select color images that have bright highlights and deep shadows.

2.   Using a soft brush, gently paint a thin, smooth coat of acrylic painting medium on the surface of the image (Figure 5.12). Do not apply a thick coat or scrub and work over the surface more than necessary. A coat that is too thick will penetrate into the paper beneath, making it difficult to remove the paper. Too much working over the surface can cause the clay to dissolve, resulting in smearing of the image.

3.   After the first coat is completely dry, apply a second coat. This can be brushed on more heavily and worked more without fear of damaging the ink. Repeat this process until about six layers have been built up. Make sure each layer is dry before applying the next.

4. Allow to dry thoroughly. There should be no haziness to the acrylic coating. When dry, dampen the back of the image with a sponge or wet towel, and float the image face up in a tray of warm water. Try not to get water on the acrylic side. When saturated with water, it tends to be more fragile.

5. After about fifteen minutes, remove the image from the water and place it face down on a smooth, clean surface. Gently, with a fingernail or a stencil knife, try to work a corner of the paper free from the acrylic emulsion (Figure 5.13). If it resists, sponge warm water onto the paper. The paper usually comes away cleanly without tearing or fraying. Some papers tend to separate leaving a layer of paper attached. If this is the case, gently rub with a finger to remove the paper.

6. Gently wash the back of the lift transfer and leave in place until the back takes on a chalky appearance. Some people recommend washing off the chalky clay coating, but I have found that doing so decreases the opacity of the dark areas. With color photo images the clay seems to have little effect.

7. Gently peel the lift transfer off the surface and lay face up for a few minutes, but return to a face-down position before the edges curl very much. Do not leave it face down indefinitely at this point or you may find the lift transfer has transferred permanently to a new surface.

8. Once dry, the lift transfer may be used as a positive. It can be used either face up or face down during exposure, but if a thick acrylic layer was built up it will work better when the clay side is in contact with the stencil. Unfortunately, this produces a mirror image.

9. To increase the durability of the lift transfer, you can laminate it to a piece of clear or matte acetate. Brush a thin coat of acrylic medium onto the acetate and immediately place the transfer on top. Roll out firmly with a soft brayer and tape down to a flat surface to dry (Figure 5.14). Because of the thickness of the acetate, it is recommended that the lift transfer side be in contact with the photo stencil during exposure.

DRYPOINT POSITIVES

A positive that has exceedingly fine lines and resembles an etching or a drypoint can be made easily as follows. Using an etching or a lithographer's needle, scratch a drawing directly into a thin but rigid

5.13   Paper being peeled off the lift transfer.

5.14   Rolling lift transfer onto the acetate while the painting medium is still wet. Air bubbles are deflated with a pin.

5.15 Rubbing ink into the scratched design.

5.16 Removing excess ink from the surface with a clean cloth.

5.17 The prepared drypoint positive (left) and the original drawing.

piece of acetate or acrylic plastic. Do not use anything thinner than 10 mils or thicker than $\frac{1}{16}$ inch. A simple needle can be made by inserting a small finishing nail into the end of a $\frac{1}{4}$-inch dowel stick and sharpening it to a fine point.

When the drawing is complete, rub opaque red or black printing ink into all the lines (Figure 5.15). Then wipe the ink off the surface using etcher's tarlatan, gauze or cotton (Figure 5.16), taking care not to remove the ink from the lines. The disadvantage of this technique is that unwanted scratches cannot be removed (Figures 5.17 and 5.18).

COMBINED TECHNIQUES

You can, of course, combine the techniques of making positives. Photo or film positives can be drawn on with photo opaque, and special effects can be created by scratching and scraping the emulsion. You can tape various positives together with cellophane tape to achieve just about any combination of graphic effects desired. The rub-down and dry-transfer materials can be applied to film positives and to lift transfers. Various moiré patterns can be created by superimposing rub-down patterns (Figure 5.19).

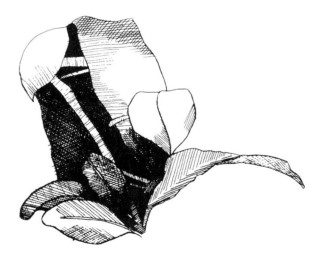

5.18 Print made from the drypoint positive.

5.19 Print made from a handmade positive in which a variety of techniques was employed. The black outline was done in photo opaque. The dot patterns are rub-down material. The hands were a lift transfer. The letters were dry-transfer material. And the wood texture was a resist stencil printed directly onto the acetate.

6.

photo stencil tec

nniques: the stencil

Once you have the positive on hand, the photo stencil itself may be prepared. At this point, the student usually experiences some trepidation, for the photo stencil permits less latitude for error than other stencils. There will be more waste of materials, some of it deliberate, as you learn to handle the photo stencil. Test strips, multiple exposures, and plain mistakes will account for most of this. All is not lost, however, for the purpose of the waste is to ensure that you have the best possible stencil. In no case should you settle for second best, for that will ensure an unsatisfying, second-best print.

There are two ways to make a photo stencil: directly and indirectly. In the direct method the stencil is made on the screen. In the indirect method the stencil is made separately and then adhered to the screen.

Artists have strong feelings about which method is best, and needless to say, sometimes irrationality tinges their discussion.

All the direct methods are basically the same. A liquid emulsion is treated to become light-sensitive, the screen is then coated, exposed, and washed out.

There are two different approaches to the indirect method. In one, a presensitized film is used; in the other, a film that needs to be sensitized prior to exposure is used.

In the case of presensitized films, the materials are ready for exposure as they come from the manufacturer. The unsensitized ones vary widely in the kind of pre-exposure preparation necessary. Some are sensitized and adhered to the screen prior to exposure, others are sensitized, dried, and exposed, and still others are sensitized, laminated to an additional plastic or paper support, and exposed while still wet.

CONTACT OR EXPOSURE FRAMES

Regardless of the type of photo stencil one uses, contact between the stencil and the positive must be as tight as possible during exposure. Poor contact can result in the loss of fine detail and the crumbling of the edges of shapes (Figure 6.1).

Vacuum pouches or frames are unsurpassed for establishing the necessary contact, and commercial processors use such equipment exclusively. In such a system the stencil and the positive are placed together in a frame, and the air is evacu-

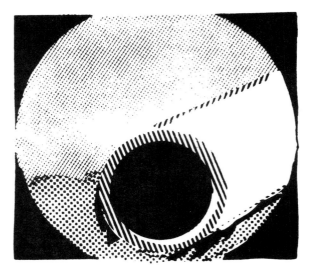

6.1   Loss of fine detail as a result of poor contact during exposure.

ated, sucking them together into perfect contact (Figure 6.2).

However, fairly simple pressure contact systems can work exceptionally well, especially with stencils smaller than 18″ x 24″. In a pressure contact system, the stencil and the positive are sandwiched together between a piece of glass and

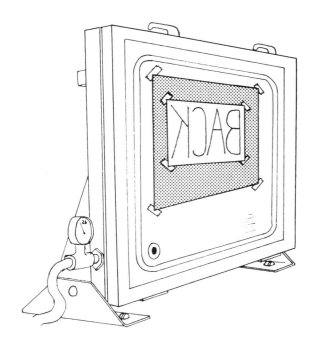

6.2   A typical table-top vacuum frame.

Masonite or wood and brought into tight contact by clamping or weighting down. To distribute the pressure uniformly over the stencil, a pad of foam rubber is placed between the stencil and the backboard.

The components of the simplest unit are: ¼-inch thick glass, 2-inch thick foam slightly smaller than the glass and a ¼-inch Masonite the same size as the glass. If the foam is white urethane, a sheet of black paper is inserted between the stencil and the foam to prevent backflash, which causes undercutting of the stencil. Pressure is created by compressing the foam and using 2-inch masking tape to tape the glass to the backboard (Figure 6.3).

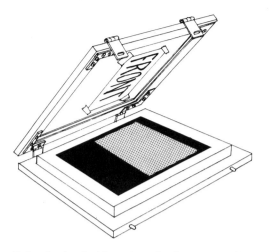

6.4　A simple hinged contact pressure frame. The block in the center is a piece of urethane foam 1 or 2 inches thick.

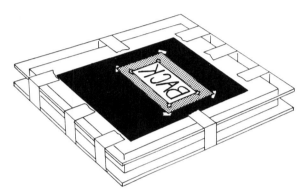

6.3　The simplest pressure contact system composed of (from top) a glass plate, the positive, stencil film, black paper, foam block, and board, all taped together.

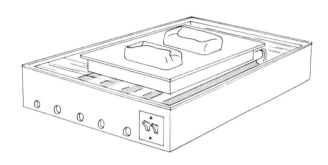

6.5　A simple homemade fluorescent light box showing cloth-covered bricks and board weighing down foam block on top of stencil film and positive.

A slightly more sophisticated contact frame requires that the glass be framed in wood or metal and hinged to a piece of ½-inch thick plywood with sufficient space between the two to accommodate the compressed foam. A simple latch can be made with a small padlock hasp (Figure 6.4).

If you are using a light table for exposure, the foam and backboard can be laid on top and weighted down with cloth-covered bricks (Figure 6.5).

Direct-emulsion screen stencils pose certain problems because the screen frame itself must be accommodated in the exposure contact frame. If you are not using a flexible plastic pouch and vacuum pump, the best method is to work with a light table for exposure with the weighted contact method above. The backboard and foam must be small enough to fit within the screen frame (Figure 6.6).

When this is not practical, place the backboard on a table, and on it place a

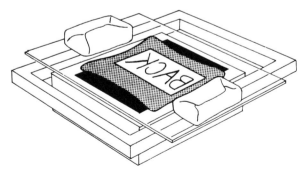

6.6　Simplest pressure contact system for use with direct-emulsion stencils. Composed of (from top) cloth-covered bricks, glass plate, positive, coated screen, black paper, and foam block.

block of foam that fits within the screen but is at least ½ inch thicker than the frame. The screen is placed over the foam and a piece of ¼-inch glass is weighted down on top. The exposure light is then suspended from above.

EXPOSURE UNITS

Practically all photo stencil materials available today have the same light requirements—the blue and ultraviolet end of the spectrum—and are relatively insensitive to other portions of the spectrum. They may be handled with reasonable confidence under subdued incandescent light. But all such materials are adversely affected by heat. These two factors require that an appropriate light source be used to expose the stencil.

ARC LAMPS

Most manufacturers discuss their photo stencil materials in terms of exposure by arc lamp, which is the standard equipment in most commercial work. An arc lamp works on a simple principle: an electric current jumping between two carbon rods produces an intensely bright spark that is particularly high in ultraviolet light (Figure

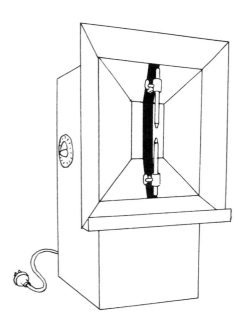

6.7   A typical 15-amp arc lamp.

6.7). The intensity of the light is a direct function of the current (amperage) passing between the carbon rods. A 15-amp unit puts out less light than a 90-amp unit.

The arc lamp is very nearly a point source of light. The absence of scattering means that exposures are short, and very fine detail is retained.

Arc lamps do have disadvantages. They generate considerable heat, so that even a 15-amp unit must be at least 30 inches from the contact frame. A 90-amp unit may have to be placed 9 feet away. The lamps also present safety hazards. The user can be severely burned if he changes the rods or readjusts them while they are hot. Severe burns of the retina can result if the arc is viewed while the lamp is on, and such burns can occur even when only the reflection is seen in the glass of the vacuum frame. Finally, because of the electrical requirements, even the smallest units require their own circuit to prevent blown fuses or overheated wiring. Safety demands that arc lamps be used with great caution.

FLUORESCENT LIGHTS

Until recently artists generally assumed that to get exposures with fluorescent light comparable to those from arc lamps, the very expensive black light (ultraviolet) tubes had to be used. Today ordinary daylight or cool white tubes are used in various arrangements as exposure units.

Fluorescent lights have many advantages. They operate at cool temperatures, permitting exposures within 4 inches of the stencil. They thus take less space than an arc lamp and a vacuum frame. The tubes have long lives and are readily available. The requirements of current can be considerably less than those of arc lamps; they rarely require separate circuitry. They can be incorporated into a unit designed to serve also as a light table for the preparation of positives. Finally, a relatively inexpensive unit tailored to your needs can be built easily. All that is required is enough channel fixtures to fill the exposure area, a box to hold them, a fitted glass or plastic top, and the wiring and switches.

There are also disadvantages. The size of the area that one can expose is only as large as the exposure unit itself. And because the tubes put out a diffused light, fine halftone detail may be lost.

PHOTO FLOODLIGHTS
AND TUNGSTEN LIGHTS

The photo floodlights commonly used for color photography can be used for exposure as well. By far the cheapest light source (at least initially), they are readily available at photo supply stores. Generally, #2 reflector photo floods are used because less light is wasted. For only occasional work on a small scale (8″ x 10″), they are more than adequate—provided one takes note of their disadvantages.

Since photo floods generate considerable heat, they require up to three feet between stencil and light. (Because of the heat, these bulbs must be used only in ceramic fixtures.) Their useful life is short —about eight hours—after which the exposure time must be increased by 50 percent for each additional hour of use. The element is much more fragile than that found in ordinary tungsten lights and is easily broken when turned off and still hot.

The photo floodlight is the only tungsten light that may be used for exposure. All others, such as household light bulbs, are deficient in blue and ultraviolet.

HALOGEN LIGHTS

Increasingly in the last ten years, halogen lights have been used in applications requiring intense light. Most sunlamps now utilize a mercury vapor light. Many slide and movie projectors use quartz iodide lights. And the newer movie lights use quartz iodide as well.

The advantage to the artist is that these lights put out considerable quantities of ultraviolet light. Quartz iodide lights are considered a point source of light, which makes them desirable for fine detail. However, they generate much heat and have a relatively short life. Mercury vapor lights (Figure 6.8) generate a more diffused light, but have a quite long, useful life and operate at cooler temperatures. Both tend to be costly.

SCREEN
PREPARATION

A clean screen in good condition, important with any stencil technique, is doubly important with photo stencils. Since all methods are water based, all grease must be removed from the screen.

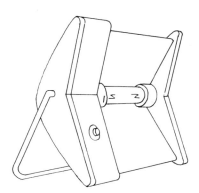

6.8   A typical mercury vapor sunlamp suitable for exposing photo stencil materials.

If a silk or dacron screen is reasonably free from ink stains, scrubbing the screen with lacquer thinner or acetone will be sufficient to open up the threads and remove grease. If the screen is old or heavily charged with ink stains, then it is advisable to follow the lacquer thinner scrubbing with a wash either in a mild kitchen cleanser (chlorine-free) or in a solution of trisodium phosphate. When using the kitchen cleanser, do not scrub with a brush, as this causes pumice particles to become embedded in the fabric and excessively frays the threads. With trisodium phosphate 1 tablespoon is dissolved in 1 quart of water, and the screen is washed with a cloth or brush. With either, the screen must be thoroughly rinsed and allowed to air-dry.

Nylon or other monofilaments must be prepped to be made receptive to the water-charged stencil. A solution of 5 percent acetic acid (white vinegar) is used to wash both sides of the screen, after which it is rinsed in cold water and allowed to air-dry.

Acetic acid performs several functions: It removes the polish from the fibers, making them receptive to the stencil emulsion. It degreases the screen and acidifies it, ensuring that indirect stencils will lie flat until dry and that the direct emulsion will retain a thin uniform film without crawling.

INDIRECT METHODS
OF PREPARING
PHOTO STENCILS

From this point, indirect and direct photo stencil techniques diverge, requiring different materials, equipment, and procedures.

NATURE OF THE MATERIALS

All indirect materials consist of a thin emulsion laminated to a plastic or paper support. They yield superior stencils when the artist is working with extremely fine detail. In addition, the time spent under subdued light conditions is lessened, and stencil experimentation does not tie up a screen.

Although it is difficult to generalize the requirements and procedures for the various indirect materials, they are roughly the same for all. The differences and the specific precautions for each will be noted in the discussions of individual materials.

STENCIL PACK-UP

As with knife-cut stencils, all types of indirect photo stencils require good contact between the stencil and the screen fabric during adhesion. The pack-up, as before, may be a piece of ¼-inch Masonite or plywood that is large enough to accommodate the stencil but smaller than the inside dimensions of the screen. Glass, of the same size and thickness, has its merits in photo stencil work, since it permits positioning the stencil over a previously printed color prior to adhesion.

EXPOSURE: GENERAL PROCEDURE

To achieve the best, repeatable results with all indirect materials, follow this exposure set-up:

1. Clean both sides of the glass in the contact frame.
2. Tape the positive to the inside of the glass with the emulsion or drawn side away from the glass. If you wish a mirror image, tape the positive with the emulsion toward the glass.

    If the glass has scratches, turn it to place them on the side opposite the positive, and position them in nonprinting areas of the stencil. (On the outside, scratches block the light, causing lines that print; on the inside, they scatter light.)
3. Turn off fluorescent lights and close window blinds.
4. If presensitized film is used, cut from the roll a piece about 2 inches bigger on all sides than the positive. Return the roll to the tube and close it.
5. Tape the sensitized stencil film over the positive with the emulsion side away from the positive (Figure 6.9).

6.9 Photo stencil film being taped over and with its base in contact with the positive.

Exposing through the base is essential with all indirect stencils, since the layer of emulsion that becomes exposed first is the one in contact with the backing sheet. Thus, regardless of the length of exposure, the stencil will not lift off inadvertently during wash-out.

6. If you are using a pressure contact frame, place the foam pad behind the stencil. Make sure the foam is at least as large as the stencil. If the foam is white urethane, insert a sheet of black paper between the stencil and the foam to prevent the light from bouncing off the foam onto the underside of the stencil, which can cause loss of fine detail.
7. Close the frame and establish good, tight contact between the positive and the stencil (Figure 6.10). The foam should be one fourth to one third thinner after compression.
8. Position the light at the appropriate distance from the contact frame. It should be centered, shining at right angles to the frame. If you are using a mercury vapor sunlamp, a distance of 2 feet is sufficient for stencil sizes up to 18″ x 24″. A 15-amp arc lamp should be from 2¼ to 3 feet away. Fluorescent lights can be as close as 4 inches.
9. Turn on the exposure light. (Avoid looking directly at the light from sunlamps or arc lamps at any time.) You can learn

6.10 Contact pressure frame being taped closed. The compression of the foam causes the Masonite backboard to bend.

to judge the proper gap between the rods of an arc lamp by observing the ambient light on a nearby wall. Mercury vapor lights require a few seconds to reach peak light output.

10. Time the exposure using a clock with a sweep second hand.

If you are using new equipment or unfamiliar materials for the first time, make test exposures. Using strips of tape or a piece of heavy cardboard larger than the stencil, progressively block out more of the stencil at regular intervals (Figure 6.11). The resulting stencil will be made up of strips that have been exposed for different periods. After development and wash-out, select the strips that have clear printing areas and solid nonprinting areas. The range of exposure times for these strips will reveal the latitude for exposure of that particular stencil under those conditions. The shorter exposure will print fine detail better, and the longer exposure will hold up better for long printing runs.

11. When the exposure times run to around ten to fifteen minutes, use that time to prepare for development and wash-out, since delay between the end of the exposure and the beginning of development is not advised. If absolutely necessary, an exposed stencil can be stored in a lightproof tube for fifteen to twenty minutes. Beyond this, the exposed particles of the emulsion react with unexposed particles, causing them to behave as if they were exposed as well.

DEVELOPMENT

The primary function of development is to complete the hardening effect of the light on the sensitized stencil. Without development, the exposed areas of most films remain water soluble.

Most stencils can be developed either by immersing them in a tray of the appropriate developer or by working small quantities of developer over the surface of the emulsion.

One uses a tray that is large enough to accommodate the stencil and enough developer to immerse the stencil. The stencil is placed emulsion-side up, and the tray is gently rocked to ensure uniform development (Figure 6.12). Slightly under-

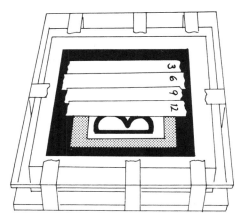

6.11 Placement of tape over stencil during exposure to determine proper exposure time. The numbers indicate how many minutes each strip was exposed.

6.12 A stencil being developed by immersing it in a tray of the appropriate developer and rocking the tray gently for the prescribed time.

sized trays or lesser amounts of developer can be used if the rocking of the tray keeps all portions of the stencil constantly wet with developer.

With the nontray method, sometimes called the puddle method, an upside-down tray or similar surface is used. The film is placed emulsion-side up and a small pool of developer is poured in the center and spread over the entire stencil with the hand (Figure 6.13). Small quantities of developer are added periodically and spread to keep the stencil thoroughly wet during development. The advantage here is that large quantities of developer do not have to be mixed and stored, so reducing costs and handling problems.

6.14   Washing out stencil immediately after development.

6.13   Developing a photo stencil by pouring a small puddle of developer in the center and rubbing it over the surface.

WASH-OUT

Immediately after development, the film must be washed out. (Certain materials not requiring development are washed out after exposure.) The most common method uses a fine, sharp spray of water at an appropriate temperature (discussed with specific materials below). The stencil is placed emulsion-side up on a smooth, elevated surface, such as an upside-down developing tray, and sprayed continuously and uniformly until all printing areas are completely free of emulsion (Figure 6.14).

Emulsions that are particularly tough can be rubbed gently with the fingertips to remove stubborn spots. Extremely fragile emulsions are easily destroyed if touched while wet. If rubbing is employed, take care to avoid scratching the emulsion with a fingernail.

In most cases water temperature is important. Water that is too hot can melt the stencil away completely. Water that is too cold will not clear the printing areas sufficiently. In addition, if too much time is spent in washing out, the stencil may lift off the backing sheet altogether.

As soon as the stencil is clear, a cold water spray is used to chill the stencil, reduce its swollen condition, and prevent accidental smearing of the stencil during adhesion.

ADHESION

For practically all indirect stencils the method of adhesion is the same. A suitable pack-up is placed under the screen, the stencil is positioned emulsion-side up on it (Figure 6.15), and the screen is lowered and weighted down.

If ¼-inch glass is used as a pack-up, a copy of the previously printed color is placed in the registration tabs beneath the glass. The stencil is placed on the glass and slid around until it is registered with the print below. (Because glass refracts light and can play visual tricks, take care to inspect the position of the stencil by looking straight down from the center.)

Adhesion takes place as soon as the screen comes in contact with the stencil. Clean, unpolished newsprint or folded paper toweling is used to blot up the excess water (Figure 6.16). This speeds the

6.15 Placing the developed stencil on a ¼-inch Masonite pack-up.

drying of the stencil and reduces chances that the stencil will bleed. The pad of toweling or newsprint must be turned or replaced frequently as it becomes stained with emulsion, to prevent redepositing the emulsion in printing areas of the stencil. Do not apply pressure during the blotting, because it can cause pinholes in the stencil, and rubbing should be avoided because it can smear the stencil.

6.16 Excess water being blotted off with a pad of paper toweling.

The screen is now left in position until dry, which is, for practical purposes, until it reaches room temperature. This will depend on atmospheric conditions and the nature of the stencil, though a fan will accelerate the process.

BACKING-SHEET REMOVAL

When the stencil is dry, the backing sheet must be removed. Some have a waxlike adhesive, others are held in place only by the surface tension of the two materials. Pushing with a finger into the screen fabric from the squeegee side at an edge of the stencil will disengage the backing sheet, which can then be pulled slowly off the stencil (Figure 6.17). The feeling of resistance should resemble that of a charge of static electricity. If the sheet pulls at the stencil, or the stencil comes off with the backing sheet or seems rubbery, then either the stencil is not dry or the screen was not properly cleaned in the beginning.

6.17 Peeling the backing sheet off the dry stencil.

STENCIL REMOVAL

Practically all indirect stencils are removed from the screen in the same way. Indirect stencils are protein gelatin emulsions that through chemical conversion become relatively impervious to water after exposure and development. What is needed is something to destroy the long protein chains and the bond between the emulsion and the screen fabric. Enzyme cleaners of various kinds are the answer. These literally digest the protein, leaving a water-soluble residue (Figure 6.18).

6.18   The effect of the enzyme on the stencil.

Though some enzyme cleaners are recommended for use in a water solution that is brushed onto the screen, most can be sprinkled in dry form on both sides of a wet stencil. After the cleanser has been allowed to stand for up to half an hour, a hot water spray is used to remove all traces of the stencil.

To speed the action of the enzyme and make it more effective, the screen must be free of any ink or block-out before the enzyme is applied. Soaking the screen in hot water before applying the enzyme also aids in removal of the stencil. Very old stencils will frequently require a second application of enzyme to remove all traces of the stencil.

A note of caution: It is particularly important that any hide glue block-out be completely removed before the enzyme is applied. Contact between the hide glue and an enzyme can result in a completely insoluble film. And commercial water-soluble block-outs should be removed with **cold** water before hot water is used, for the same reason.

After the screen is clear of the stencil, it must be washed in a mild acid solution to kill the enzyme and prevent any residue

from attacking future stencils. A cloth soaked in white vinegar and applied to both sides of the screen will do this effectively. After the vinegar wash, rinse the screen in cold water and allow it to air-dry.

Enzyme cleaner can be stored for considerable periods of time if it is kept relatively cool and away from moisture and acidic atmospheres.

TYPES OF INDIRECT PHOTO STENCILS

UNSENSITIZED STENCILS: CARBON TISSUE

Although not used as much today as a decade or two ago, carbon tissue is still considered by many to be the superior method for the reproduction of fine detail. Although the principle was known in the 1860s, it was not until the 1920s that it began to be employed in photographic silkscreen. For the next forty years it reigned as the standard to which all other materials were compared. The name itself comes from the early use of carbon as a pigment in the emulsion. It is still the cheapest photo stencil material, and it can be stored almost indefinitely.

The basics of working with any unsensitized material can be learned from the carbon tissue method. Certain brands of film handle somewhat differently, but the overall procedure is the same. The reader can thereby decide for himself whether this is a direction he wishes to pursue.

Carbon tissue films have a gelatin emulsion that has been laminated to a paper backing sheet. They are sensitized by immersing them in a 2 to 4 percent solution of potassium or ammonium bichromate in water (3 to 7 tablespoons per quart). The temperature of this solution during sensitization should be between 45 and 65 degrees Fahrenheit. (The cooler the solution, the shorter the exposure.) Immersion should last for one to three minutes, but no longer, or the next step will be difficult.

The now sensitized film is next squeegeed with a piece of cardboard, emulsion-side down, onto a sheet of 5-mil clear polyester, mylar or vinyl plastic (Figure 6.19). Cleaning the polyester with turpentine before the squeegeeing facilitates separation of stencil from this support after the stencil

6.19 Squeegeeing the sensitized carbon tissue onto a piece of plastic with a piece of cardboard.

is adhered to the screen. Other plastics will need to be waxed and polished to permit their removal after adhesion. If you use a cool sensitizing solution, the plastic support should also be cooled before squeegeeing the emulsion to it. Excess sensitizer should be removed from the plastic and the backing sheet.

Exposure, with the plastic support facing the light source, is next. The times can only be approximated here because many variables are involved, but a 15-amp arc lamp will require an exposure of about twelve to fifteen minutes at 30 inches.

After exposure, the stencil is immersed in a tray of water at between 100 and 110 degrees (Figure 6.20). When the emul-

sion begins to ooze out from between the paper backing sheet and the plastic support, the backing sheet is gently peeled away (Figure 6.21). Continue to gently rock the tray until all printing areas are free of emulsion.

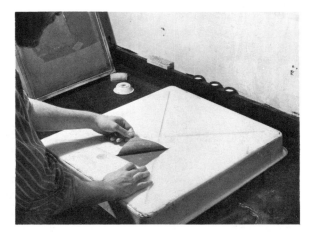

6.21 Peeling the paper backing off the carbon tissue.

The stencil is next transferred to a tray of cool water (between 60 and 70 degrees) to reduce swelling and to harden, for not more than four minutes.

(Many types of carbon tissue can also be processed with the spray method rather than the tray method. Instead of soaking, water of the appropriate temperature is sprayed onto the paper backing until it can be separated. Spraying is continued until the printing areas are free of emulsion (Figure 6.22). A cold water spray follows.)

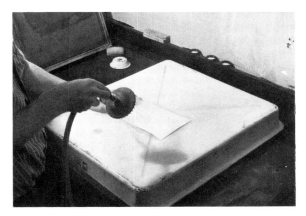

6.20 Soaking the paper backing of the carbon tissue to permit its being peeled from the emulsion attached to the plastic sheet.

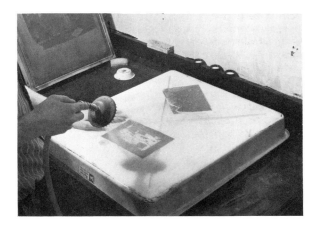

6.22 Washing out the carbon tissue stencil after the paper backing has been removed.

The developed stencil is adhered as described on p. 90. When the stencil is dry the plastic support is removed.

As noted earlier, all bichromate-sensitized materials can be handled under subdued incandescent light, and they are least sensitive when wet.

To avoid difficulty in removing the backing sheet, some artists sponge isopropyl alcohol onto the paper backing before development.

Carbon tissues that come with a plastic backing, instead of paper, must have a paper backing laminated to the emulsion during sensitization. The plastic then serves the same function as the plastic support described above.

PRESENSITIZED STENCILS

The best-known presensitized photo stencil films are Ulano, McGraw, and Autotype. All three manufacturers produce a wide range of materials, both sensitized and unsensitized.

Using presensitized films has its advantages, especially if you are working casually with a small operation. Such films are ready for exposure directly from the manufacturer, and the results tend to be better and more reliable than unsensitized film. They also eliminate the need for preparing bichromate solutions and preserving them for future use.

There are disadvantages also. Presensitized stencils cost more than direct-emulsion or unsensitized stencils, and there is no way to vary the sensitivity of the emulsion.

In my work with McGraw Colorgraph 4570, Ulano's Hi Fi Green and Blue Poly, and Autotype's Super Star #1, I have found that all are excellent products. If you live in or near a metropolitan area, you will probably be able to obtain them easily. If not, one of them should be available near where you live. The following sections will provide you with sufficient understanding of the differences and similarities of these materials. You should then be able to decide what other materials might serve you just as well.

Autotype Super Star #1

Autotype Super Star #1 is particularly easy to work with and allows much flexibility in working conditions. For the beginner or casual worker with photo stencil, these qualities can be particularly useful.

Emulsion: This film produces a thin, tough stencil with short exposures. It does not seem to swell much during development.

Screen Preparation: The manufacturer recommends using well-cleaned and degreased screens, but any reasonably clean screen adheres well. Since Super Star #1 is particularly thin, a 16xx screen (or the equivalent) is recommended to minimize sawtooth edges. It adheres well to both multifilaments and monofilaments.

Exposure: The speed is comparable to McGraw Colorgraph 4570, and the film can be exposed with any of the units described earlier. The emulsion does not become sticky when exposed to considerable heat. Exposure is two minutes with a 15-amp arc lamp at 30 inches, and ten minutes with a mercury vapor sunlamp at 2 feet.

Development: The manufacturer recommends a one-to-four, 20-volume hydrogen peroxide and water solution for one minute by the tray method.

Straight 3 percent hydrogen peroxide can be used in the puddle method without timing, by using the following procedure. Place the film, after exposure, emulsion-side (dull side) up on an elevated flat surface. Pour a puddle of 3 percent hydrogen peroxide in the center and spread it over the stencil. At first the film will feel slippery, but after a few seconds you will feel resistance. The surface of the film will become milky at about the time resistance is noticed. Continue development until this milky surface is loosened from the stencil. Toward the end of development, take care to spread the developer from the center outward to prevent abrading the emulsion from the backing sheet.

Washout: A strong, sharp spray of water at 105 to 110 degrees is used to wash out the stencil immediately after development. Since the film is comparatively tough, the spray can be quite forceful. Although not generally recommended, water temperatures can be as low as 95 degrees, but considerable rubbing with the hand may be necessary.

When wash-out is begun, it will seem at first as if nothing is happening, but then the water as it runs off will bear a reddish tinge. A few seconds longer and the reddish tinge deepens, and the image appears. Keep spraying continuously over the stencil until all printing areas are clear. Any stubborn areas can be rubbed with the fingertips, but keep the spray moving while doing this. If, while rubbing, you notice adjacent areas becoming lighter, you are rubbing too hard or too much. If the edges of shapes start to crumble or lift off, you have spent too much time washing out. If the stencil begins to melt, the wash-out water is too hot.

In addition to the cold water rinse after wash-out, the stencil can be flooded with a 50 percent isopropyl alcohol solution to speed the drying and further reduce the risk of smearing the stencil during adhesion.

Adhesion: Follow the procedure described on p. 90. Since Super Star #1 has a very thin plastic backing sheet, the stencil should be held by adjacent corners when you are carrying it from sink to worktable; otherwise it may fold on itself and be ruined. And because the emulsion is thin, less of it is picked up on the toweling or newsprint used in blotting.

Printing: This film prints fine detail very well because of the thin emulsion. Partic-ularly thin emulsions (short exposures) will wear and develop pinholes from vigorous scrubbing with clean-up solvents, especially when used on fabrics coarser than 16xx.

Screen Recovery: If a Super Star #1 sten-cil is removed within twenty-four hours, a very strong spray of 120-degree water will usually remove it completely. If it has been left on the screen for a few weeks, one or two applications of an enzyme cleaner will be necessary.

Storage: Stencils may be left on the screen indefinitely. The unused roll can be stored for months with no drying out or decreased sensitivity to light.

Ulano Hi Fi Green and Blue Poly

Ulano Hi Fi Green and Blue Poly are very reliable films of high quality and ease of use, yielding good, durable stencils for the artist. But as these films are less tolerant of variations in procedure, you must follow directions carefully.

Emulsion: Hi Fi Green has a thick emulsion that swells considerably during develop-ment and wash-out. The backing sheet is a 5-mil translucent vinyl. Blue Poly has an extremely thin emulsion that also swells and softens considerably during develop-ment and wash-out. It is available with either a 2- or 3-mil clear polyester backing sheet.

Screen Requirements and Preparation: Because the emulsion is thick, Hi Fi Green may be used effectively with 12xx or equivalent meshes. Blue Poly works better with 16xx or finer meshes. Any fabric can be used, and no special preparation is needed.

Exposure: These films have similar ex-posure characteristics and require about twice the exposure time of Autotype Super Star #1 or McGraw Colorgraph 4570. Any of the light sources described can be used, although this film becomes quite tacky under hot lights. In that case a fan should also be used. A 15-amp arc lamp at 30 inches will require an exposure of five to six minutes. A mercury vapor sunlamp at 2 feet will require an exposure of about twenty minutes.

Development: The manufacturer recom-mends and sells a two-part developer in dry form that can be dissolved in water as needed. Because the emulsion becomes particularly soft, tray development is also recommended.

Prepare the developer before exposure by mixing 1 ounce of part A and 1 ounce of part B with 16 ounces of 65 to 70 degree water. Colder temperatures result in poor penetration of the developer, and warmer temperatures cause the emulsion to become too soft. Agitate the solution until all crystals are dissolved.

This solution is good for one working day. No attempt should be made to save or store it because poisonous gases are formed. After using the developer for the first time, cover it with an opaque lid, as exposure to light causes it to decompose rapidly.

After exposure, immerse the film emul-sion-side up in the developer and agitate it by rocking the try for 2½ minutes. (The manufacturer recommends a minimum of 1½ minutes.) If the water is hard, you may have to increase the time, unless you use distilled water. Too much develop-ment, however, can cause the emulsion to lift off the backing sheet. No change is apparent in the stencil during development, although the developer turns yellow.

Alternate Development: Recently another artist told me that using 1½ percent hydro-gen peroxide yielded good results when the film was immersed for two to three minutes. Since I find large trays of de-velopers a nuisance and dislike mixing solutions, I experimented with 3 percent hydrogen peroxide using the puddle method and timing development for one minute. The results were very good. The drawback was that the emulsion became exceedingly soft, requiring the use of a fairly large quantity of peroxide and the gentlest movement over the surface of the film, or the emulsion tended to rub away completely.

Wash-Out: Water temperature is critical with these films. A fairly gentle but fine spray between 92 and 96 degrees is used. Too strong or too coarse a spray can cause melting, lifting, or pounding off of the emulsion. The wash-out should be as rapid as possible, the spray continually moving over the stencil. If stubborn areas require rubbing, do so extremely gently. Avoid any rubbing in areas with fine dots or lines of emulsion since they will rub away easily. This film in particular requires immediate rinsing with cold water to prevent smearing during adhesion.

Adhesion: These films adhere easily, but care must be used not to blot too hard because of the soft, easily smeared emulsions.

Printing: These stencils hold up well in printing, especially the Hi Fi Green. They have good resistance to solvents.

Storage: Once on the screen, these stencils may be left there indefinitely. Unused film should be kept tightly sealed in its original wrapping and tube to prevent its drying out and lifting off the backing sheet.

Recovery: This stencil can usually be removed with 120-degree water even if it has been on the screen for some time. Enzyme cleaners are used to remove any stubborn spots of emulsion.

McGraw Colorgraph 4570

This film is particularly well suited to the artist who wishes relatively high speed (short exposure) and ease in processing.

Emulsion: This film has a fairly thick and tough emulsion on a 5-mil plastic support. If stored below 60 degrees and used within six months, it is self-developing.

Exposure: Exposure characteristics are similar to Autotype Super Star #1. Because the emulsion does become somewhat tacky when exposed to hot light sources, a fan should be used during exposure. When using a 15-amp arc lamp, an exposure of two to three minutes is required. With a mercury vapor lamp at 24 inches, an exposure of ten to twelve minutes is needed.

Development: Because of its self-developing properties, Colorgraph 4570 can be washed out directly after exposure with a strong, sharp spray of water at 105 to 115 degrees.

If the film has passed its expiration date or has been stored at temperatures above 60 degrees, hydrogen peroxide development will be needed. The manufacturer recommends 0.5 percent hydrogen peroxide as a developer, using either the tray or puddle method for two minutes. My experience has shown that 3 percent hydrogen peroxide works just as well with the puddle method. Since the film undergoes no visible change during development, it is important to time development for two minutes. If you have problems with the film lifting off the backing sheet, use a weaker peroxide solution.

Wash-out: This stencil film washes out easily and rapidly with a fine, sharp spray at 105 to 115 degrees. It is tough enough to withstand considerable rubbing with fingertips to clear stubborn spots.

If you use the self-developing properties and notice during wash-out that the clear areas remain clogged and nonprinting areas wash out, the film has expired and should be developed prior to wash-out. The expiration of the self-developing property does not affect the speed of the film.

Adhesion: This film adheres easily by blotting, and no particular precautions need be taken.

Printing: The stencil is durable, holding up well for long runs, and is resistant to all solvents.

Storage: As noted, the shelf life of the self-developing property is six months if stored at 60 degrees. It can be stored for prolonged periods beyond this with no detrimental effect provided that it is developed as above. Since it is susceptible to drying out and delaminating, it should be kept in a tightly closed container.

Recovery: If the stencil is removed within twenty-four hours, 120-degree water will remove it. Otherwise follow the enzyme procedure previously described.

PROBLEMS, SOLUTIONS AND PREVENTIONS: A CHECKLIST

What follows are some of the more common problems encountered when using indirect photo stencils.

1. A sawtooth effect appears at the edges of shapes after cleaning and reprinting with a second color.

    Causes: A. Clean-up solvent too strong.

                      B. Scrubbing during clean-up too vigorous.

C. Screen fabric mesh too coarse.
D. Stencil too thin.
E. Poor adhesion.

Solutions: None.
Preventions:
A. Use a milder solvent.
B. Use larger quantities of solvent and less scrubbing.
C. Use finer mesh fabrics.
D. Increase exposure time.
E. Thoroughly degrease and prep screen.

2. Black lines (clear lines in stencil) appear that are not in the positive (Figure 6.23).

6.23 **Black lines in upper right caused by scratches in the glass of the contact frame.**

Cause: Scratches in contact frame glass.
Solution: Paint them out with an appropriate block-out after the stencil is adhered.
Prevention: Turn the glass so that the scratches are on the opposite side from the positive, and try to

position them in non-printing areas.

3. Fine lines seem to be clogged with emulsion (Figure 6.24).

6.24 **The missing hairlines on some of the letters are caused by too long an exposure.**

Causes:
A. Silk too coarse.
B. Exposure too great.
C. Emulsion too swollen.
D. Improper adhesion.

Solutions: None.
Preventions:
A. Use 16xx or finer mesh.
B. Reduce exposure time.
C. Chill stencil with cold water or 50 percent solution of isopropyl alcohol after wash-out.
D. Blot gently, do not rub, with clean newsprint.

4. Texture and halftone areas are not developing (washing out) properly. Dots or textures change noticeably in size.

Causes:
A. Poor contact between positive and stencil during exposure.
B. Emulsion side of positive was not in contact with stencil during exposure.

Solutions: None.

Preventions: A. Check the contact frame to ensure that tight, uniform pressure is achieved.
              B. Make sure that the emulsion is in contact with stencil backing sheet during exposure.

5.   There is difficulty in removing photo stencil with enzyme.
     Causes: A. Stencil has been on the screen for long time.
                   B. Screen was not thoroughly cleaned after printing.
                   C. Enzyme has lost potency.
                   D. Insufficient time allowed for enzyme to work.
     Solutions: A. Repeat enzyme application and follow with a soap scrubbing.
                   B. Remove all traces of ink before using enzyme.
                   C. Use fresh enzyme and store it tightly closed.
                   D. Use sufficient enzyme and permit the screen to soak for half an hour.
     Preventions: A. Remove photo stencil as soon as possible after printing.
                   B. Wash screen in trisodium phosphate.
                   C. Store enzymes properly.
                   D. See Solution D.

6.   The stencil does not adhere well and tends to peel off the screen when dry.
     Causes: A. Multifilament screen fabric old or clogged.
                   B. Monofilament screen fabric improperly prepped.
     Solutions: None.
     Preventions: A. Clean the screen thoroughly with lacquer thinner and wash it with trisodium phosphate.
                   B. Wash the fabric with 5 percent acetic acid (white vinegar) and degrease it with trisodium phosphate.

7.   An imperfect negative stencil appears during wash-out.
     Causes: A. Failure to develop before wash-out.
                   B. Self-developing film has expired.
                   C. Exhausted developer.
     Solutions: None.
     Preventions: A. Follow developing instructions carefully.
                   B. Treat as a hydrogen peroxide developing film.
                   C. Replace developer and store it tightly sealed away from light.

8.   Pinholes are developing in the stencil (Figure 6.25).
     Causes: A. Failure to neutralize enzyme previously used.
                   B. Stencil too thin.

6.25 Pinholes in photo stencil, caused by excessive blotting, too short an exposure, too coarse a screen mesh, or dust on the screen.

6.26 Poor printing caused by a veil of emulsion left in the printing areas of the stencil.

C. Dust on stencil, positive, or glass during exposure.

Solutions: A. None.
B. Touch up the pinholes with an appropriate block-out.
C. Same as Solution B.

Preventions: A. Use white vinegar to neutralize enzyme after use.
B. Increase exposure time.
C. Clean all surfaces through which light must pass.

9. The stencil is sticking to the backing sheet and is being pulled off the screen.

Causes: A. Stencil not dry.
B. Screen improperly prepped.

Solutions: A. Allow the stencil to dry before removing the rest of the backing sheet.
B. None.

Preventions: A. Use a fan or an isopropyl alcohol wash to speed drying.
B. Thoroughly clean, degrease, and prep screens prior to adhesion.

10. Printing areas have a veil or haze of emulsion after adhesion (Figure 6.26).

Causes: A. Improper adhesion technique.
B. Improper wash-out.

Solutions: A. Rub or blot the offending areas with a damp towel after the backing sheet is removed.
B. See Solution A.

Preventions: A. Use cold water rinse and isopropyl alcohol wash after wash-out and blot gently with clean towel or newsprint.
B. Continue wash-out

until water is free
of color.

11. Printing areas have a veil or haze of emulsion after wash-out.

Causes:	A.	Film has expired.
	B.	Film stored at high temperature.
	C.	Film has been exposed to light.
Solutions:	None.	
Preventions:	A.	Store film properly and use it within a year of purchase.
	B.	Store it at temperatures below 75 degrees.
	C.	Handle·film only under subdued incandescent light.

12. Certain areas retain a noticeable film of emulsion during wash-out even though contact was good during exposure and the stencil material is fresh.

Causes:	A.	Positive insufficiently opaque.
	B.	Wash-out temperature too low.
	C.	Wash-out spray not forceful enough.
	D.	Exposure too long.
Solutions:	A.	Rub the film gently with your fingertips.
	B.	Increase the water temperature to the maximum permitted.
	C.	Increase the water pressure.
	D.	None.
Preventions:	A.	Re-opaque the offending areas.
	B.	See Solution B.
	C.	See Solution C.
	D.	Decrease the exposure time.

13. During wash-out, certain areas lift off the backing sheet.

Causes:	A.	Failure to develop correctly.
	B.	Wash-out water too hot.
	C.	Stencil film was old.
	D.	Too much time

spent in washing out.

	E.	Water spray too coarse or too weak.
Solutions:	None.	
Preventions:	A.	Follow the manufacturer's directions carefully in preparing and using the developer.
	B.	Use the minimum temperature for wash-out water.
	C.	Replace the film and store it tightly sealed.
	D.	Shorten the exposure time and wash out the film rapidly.
	E.	Use a fine, sharp water spray.

DIRECT-EMULSION PHOTO STENCILS

A great deal has been said recently about the wonders of direct emulsion. It seems to be on every artist's lips, as if it were the answer to every problem. And as if it were a radically new or better process than what has gone before.

There is no question that direct emulsion is cheaper in material cost than the indirect methods and that the stencils have much greater durability under printing conditions. But the idea that direct emulsion is easier or faster or that it yields better results is, for the most part, a popular myth, mainly perpetuated by those who are trying to sound knowledgeable about an area in which they have had little first-hand experience or, contrariwise, by those who have used it to the exclusion of other methods and so cannot claim to know them well.

As with any process, a certain amount of practice and patience is necessary in order to get a direct emulsion to work best. Anyone who is interested in photo stencils, but who plans to prepare only an occasional direct emulsion should not bother with it. Stick to other stencil processes. And if you do not have the time and the patience to experiment with direct-emulsion processes or to perfect the needed skills, still don't bother, in spite of the temptation of lower costs. Direct emulsion works best, and has greatest significance, in commercial applications.

With indirect photo stencils it was important to discuss specific brands because they vary widely. But with direct emulsions one basic method applies to all brands (with a few exceptions). Basically, all direct emulsions follow this procedure:

1. Prep the screen.
2. Prepare the stock sensitizer solution.
3. Sensitize the emulsion.
4. Coat the screen.
5. Expose the screen.
6. Wash it out.
7. Print.
8. Use bleach to remove the stencil.
9. Wash up with lacquer thinner.

This is obviously a lengthier process than is needed with a presensitized photo stencil. And not only is the total work time greater, there is more waiting between steps. Moreover, most of the work must be done under subdued incandescent lighting. In short, it takes roughly 1½ hours to prepare a direct emulsion for printing, as opposed to 20 to 30 minutes for a presensitized one.

For large-scale commercial processors, however, the direct-emulsion stencil is increasingly favored, for it is exceedingly resistant to abrasion, holding up well for long runs. It can be treated or replaced with a resist block-out or epoxy filler for even greater durability and total resistance to solvents.

Then, too, from a commercial standpoint, exposure time is not the only variable, for it is also possible to vary the sensitivity of the emulsion and its thickness. Finally, most commercial processors make several stencils at a time because of the volume of their work, and thus the time needed to make one stencil is greatly reduced.

Since most artists work alone, in an on-again, off-again manner, with less than optimal equipment and facilities, the merits of direct emulsion come into question. Those artists who are working full time, on the other hand, in all likelihood will be using the commercial processor's services in the making of direct-emulsion photo stencils.

NATURE OF THE MATERIALS

Direct-emulsion coatings are of the light-hardening kind, as are the indirect film types. Although the principle of light-hardening emulsions has been known for over a hundred years, not until after the Second World War did it come into its own.

Practically all brands are modified polyvinyls, usually polyvinyl alcohol and acetate. Like the gelatin films, they remain water-soluble until exposed to intense light or ultraviolet light. The principal sensitizers used are potassium bichromate and ammonium bichromate. These sensitizers can be used interchangeably, although the ammonium bichromate is somewhat more sensitive to light than potassium bichromate.

SCREEN PREPARATION AND REQUIREMENTS

Silk fabrics should not be used with direct emulsions unless no attempt will be made to recover the screen after use. The bleaches used to remove the emulsion will destroy the silk.

Since synthetic fabrics are by nature polished fibers and lack porosity, they must be thoroughly prepped before the emulsion is applied. (See the section on screen preparation earlier in this chapter for details.) The prepping ensures that the liquid emulsion will remain a smooth, uniform sheet once applied to the screen and will dry without crawling or causing pinholes or "fish eyes."

THE SENSITIZER

Both potassium and ammonium bichromates are available from silkscreen suppliers or from the larger photography stores. Both come in a granulated crystalline form and should be stored away from light, moisture, and heat. Both are reasonably inexpensive and available in 1 pound quantities. Since 1 pound of powder will make 1 gallon of sensitizer, and 1 gallon of sensitizer can sensitize up to 5 gallons of emulsion, you may judge your needs accordingly.

To prepare the sensitizer, slowly dissolve 4 ounces (7 to 8 tablespoons) in a quart of lukewarm water (under 90 degrees). This should be done, of course, under subdued incandescent light. If any crystals precipitate out as the solution cools, there is no problem—so long as they are kept from mixing into the emulsion.

A dark brown or green bottle, closed with a tight cap, should be used to store the sensitizer, and it should be kept in a cool, dark place and used within a couple of months. Exposed to light or heat, it loses its sensitivity.

SENSITIZING THE EMULSION

The speed or sensitivity of the emulsion can be controlled by varying the ratio of sensitizer to emulsion. Too much sensitizer, however, may cause the emulsion to become too thin for effective coating, especially with fabrics coarser than 16xx (or the equivalent). As a starter, mix 1 part of stock sensitizer solution with 5 parts of emulsion. Stir the mixture thoroughly, but do not whip it, as this creates air bubbles that will cause pinholes in the stencil. Remember, all work should be carried out only under subdued light and away from ultraviolet light sources.

Do not sensitize a larger volume of emulsion than is needed for the day's work. Since the bichromate sensitizer causes an emulsion to thin rapidly with age, it will be difficult, if not impossible, to coat a screen uniformly with a premixed emulsion.

COATING THE SCREEN

The screen is coated by spreading the emulsion over the screen in one stroke with an applicator. Though several applicators are marketed, any thin, stiff, non-porous material (metal or plastic) may be used. The applicator should be as long as the area to be coated is wide, but shorter than the inside dimension of the screen. It should be about $\frac{1}{16}$-inch thick and about 4 inches wide. A well-sharpened squeegee with a hard blade can also be used.

Place the screen on a flat surface with the printing side up. Pour a bead of emulsion along one end of the screen (Figure 6.27). Position the applicator behind the bead, leaning it forward slightly (Figure 6.28). Lift the opposite end of the screen slightly and begin to spread the emulsion (Figure 6.29). Pull the applicator steadily up to the top, maintaining firm and uniform pressure (Figure 6.30). As you near the top, with the screen in a near-vertical position, lean the applicator back slightly, and pick up the excess emulsion (Figure 6.31) and return it to its container, or use it for the other side of the screen (Figure 6.32).

Now lay the screen flat with the printing side down, but not in contact with the surface below. Pour a smaller bead on the inside and repeat the coating application. Leave the screen in a horizontal position, printing side down (but not touching), to dry. Use a fan to accelerate the drying.

The coating on the inside helps to ensure good adhesion and to prevent lifting off during wash-out, and also makes

6.27 Pouring a bead of sensitized emulsion onto underside of screen.

6.28 Applicator (squeegee) in position behind emulsion, ready to spread it across the screen.

6.29   Screen slightly elevated as squeegee spreads emulsion.

6.30   Screen raised still further as squeegee reaches the end of the stroke.

6.31   Screen now near vertical at the end of the stroke. Excess emulsion flows back onto squeegee blade, making it easy to remove.

6.32   Applying just-removed excess emulsion to the other side of the screen.

it easier to remove the unexposed emulsion from the printing areas.

When the first coat is dry, repeat the process on the printing side only. When this second coat is dry, you are ready to expose the screen.

EXPOSURE

The exposure lights previously discussed can be used with direct emulsion. However, it is more important that the exposing light be well centered and at right angles to the screen; otherwise a noticeably uneven (and often unusable) exposure may occur.

As with other materials, good, tight contact is required between the sensitized emulsion and the positive. Although most manufacturers do not recommend simple pressure contact systems, I have found that they work very well.

The simplest system consists of placing a 2-inch slab of foam, of a size that will fit within the screen frame, on a table. On this place a piece of black paper to prevent backflash. On top place the screen with the printing surface up. The positive goes emulsion-side down on the screen, and a piece of ¼-inch glass is weighted down. The light is then positioned above the screen at the appropriate distance.

Exposure time will vary from five to fifteen minutes with a mercury vapor sunlamp at about 2 feet. This considerable variation is caused by differences in the amount and type of sensitizer and by the thickness of the emulsion applied to the screen. In my experience a ten minute exposure works well with ammonium bichromate, but every artist will have to determine for himself the best exposure for the equipment and materials he is using.

DEVELOPMENT/WASH-OUT

Thoroughly wet both sides of the screen with warm water (100 to 110 degrees, but no hotter); colder water will work, but not as well. This initial soaking swells the emulsion and aids in quick and clean removal of the unexposed emulsion.

Using a strong, sharp spray, spray both sides of the screen. Avoid rubbing on the printing side. If certain areas appear not to clear, rub on the inside of the screen while spraying (Figures 6.33, 6.34 and

6.34   The screen being washed out from the printing side with minimal rubbing.

6.35   Initial spraying during wash-out, showing the emergence of the image.

6.35). At first the inside of the screen should feel slimy, but as the thin unexposed coat is removed, it should feel more like the screen fabric itself. When all printing areas are completely clear, switch to cold water, and then set the screen aside to air-dry. A fan can be used to speed drying.

6.33   With the screen elevated off the bottom of the sink, the inside of the screen is gently rubbed during wash-out to remove unexposed emulsion.

If there appears to be any veil of emulsion in the printing areas, blot gently on the inside with clean newsprint (Figure 6.36).

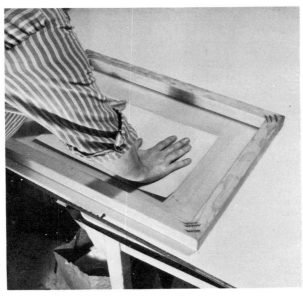

6.36 **Blotting with newsprint to remove any veil of emulsion that may remain in the printing areas.**

PROBLEMS

At this point problems will emerge or be confirmed.

1. The emulsion lifts during wash-out.
   Causes:
   - A. Failure to coat the inside of the screen.
   - B. Poorly prepped screen.
   - C. Rubbing on the printing side.
   - D. Wash-out water too hot.
   - E. Spray too coarse.
   - F. Exposure too short.

   Solutions: None.
   Preventions:
   - A. Apply thin coat of emulsion to inside during first application.
   - B. Degrease screen and wash with white vinegar.
   - C. Rub only on inside of screen.
   - D. Do not use water at temperatures above 110 degrees.

   - E. Use a fine, sharp spray.
   - F. Increase exposure time.

2. Printing areas do not clear.
   Causes:
   - A. Poorly prepped screen.
   - B. Failure to coat inside sufficiently.
   - C. Exposure too short.
   - D. Wash-out spray too weak.
   - E. Wash-out water too cool.

   Solutions: None for A, B, or C.
   D, E. See Preventions.
   Preventions:
   - A. Degrease screen and wash with white vinegar.
   - B. Apply thin coat of emulsion to inside during first application.
   - C. Increase exposure time.
   - D. Increase spray pressure.
   - E. Increase water temperature.

3. Edges of shapes have sawtooth appearance.
   Causes:
   - A. Nature of bichromate sensitizers with direct emulsions.
   - B. Screen mesh too coarse.
   - C. Poor contact between positive and emulsion.

   Solutions: None.
   Preventions:
   - A. Use an indirect method.
   - B. Use 16xx mesh or finer.
   - C. Increase pressure of contact frame.

4. Fine printing lines close up.
   Causes:
   - A. Light source too diffused.
   - B. Backflash from foam.
   - C. Exposure too long.
   - D. Poor contact between positive and emulsion.

Solutions: None.
Preventions:
A. Use an arc or quartz iodide light source.
B. Place black paper on foam.
C. Decrease exposure time.
D. Increase pressure in contact frame.

5. Fine halftone dots disappear (Figure 6.37).

6.37 Disappearance of fine halftone dots caused by:

(1) overexposure in the light areas, underexposure in the dark areas;

(2) plugging up of stencil during printing in the light areas, bleeding together during printing in the dark areas;

(3) overdevelopment or washing away in the dark areas;

(4) dots too fine for the mesh fabric being used.

Causes:
A. Screen mesh too coarse.
B. Light source too diffused.
C. Improper exposure.
D. Poor contact between positive and emulsion.
E. Excessive wash-out.

Solutions: None.
Preventions:
A. Use minimum mesh-to-halftone ratio of 3 to 1.
B. Use arc or quartz iodide light source.
C. If nonprinting dots are disappearing, increase exposure. If printing dots are disappearing, decrease exposure.
D. Increase pressure in contact frame.
E. Decrease rubbing or wash-out time.

6. Pinholes appear in the emulsion.
Causes:
A. Dust.
B. Air bubbles in the emulsion.
Solutions:
A. Paint out with left-over emulsion.
B. Same as Solution A.
Preventions:
A. After prepping of screen, allow to air-dry, do not rub dry with towel.
B. When sensitizing emulsion, stir, but do not whip.

7. Stencil breaks down during wash-out, but does not lift off.
Causes:
A. Exposure too short.
B. Improper light position.
Solutions: None.
Preventions:
A. Increase exposure time.
B. Position light in center and at right angles to screen.

STENCIL REMOVAL

As mentioned before, there is no practical way of removing the emulsion from a silk fabric without destroying the silk. Chlorine bleach is needed to break down the polymer chain of the polyvinyl into a water-soluble monomer, and bleach, unfortunately, destroys silk.

In reclaiming such synthetic fabrics as dacron, polyester, or nylon, wash both sides with hot water to swell the emulsion and aid the penetration of the bleach. Saturate both sides of the screen with the chlorine bleach and scrub briskly with a nylon brush. Continue scrubbing until some decomposition of the emulsion becomes apparent. Let the screen sit for about fifteen minutes, and then resaturate it and continue scrubbing. Continue this process until most of the emulsion has been removed. At this point use a water spray as strong and as hot as possible and thoroughly wash and scrub out the remaining emulsion.

Now examine the screen to see whether it is free and clear of any haze. If certain small areas show a faint haze, you can remove this with acetone or fast lacquer thinner. If there is considerable haze, repeat the bleach and scrubbing operation.

A more effective method of removal involves immersing the entire screen in a tray of chlorine bleach and allowing it to soak until the emulsion freely brushes away. Though the use of large amounts of bleach can cause problems in poorly ventilated areas or with very large screens, the lack of a large enough tray can be overcome. A tray can be improvised by taping

6.38   A large plastic garbage bag taped to the outside of a screen to form a tray.

a plastic garbage bag to the outside of the screen and then pouring enough bleach inside it to cover the emulsion (Figure 6.38). Since the tray and screen are now one, it is an easy task to pick up the screen and pour the bleach back into the bottle when you are finished.

As a rule, try to remove a stencil soon after you have no further use for it. The older the emulsion, the harder it becomes, requiring just that much more work later on.

7.
combined stencil

techniques

There are occasions——whether because of expediency, registration problems, or a desire to produce special effects——when two or more stencil techniques can be used to create a single stencil. On other occasions two or more techniques may be used together in order to achieve several colors in successive printings by simply altering the original stencil rather than by replacing it completely. Such combined stencil techniques are the subject of this chapter. But before going into the details, we must first describe one remaining stencil technique.

RESIST STENCILS

Resist stencil techniques are probably the most spontaneous, the most direct, and the most unforgiving of all. The resist stencil——and many times the idea for it, too——is created directly on the screen. As a result, the technical and aesthetic success of the stencil will not be known until it is printed, by which time it is too late to do anything about mistakes except to begin again.

All resist techniques rely on the incompatibility of two different materials—— the drawing materials and the stencil or block-out materials.

The most common resist stencil calls for the use of waxy drawing materials and a water-soluble block-out. The waxy materials are not affected by water and can be removed with turpentine. The block-out is unaffected by turpentine or by the ink. Lithographic tusche or silkscreen toosh, liquid latex or latex frisket materials, oil pastels, wax crayons, and lithographic pencils work very well for drawing on the screen (Figures 7.1 and 7.2).

Litho crayons come in various hardnesses, but the #2 and #3 work best. Tusche and toosh work best with a brush, but if fabrics finer than 12xx are used, they can be thinned and used in a lettering pen. Tusche is thinned with water, and toosh with turpentine.

The block-out most often used is hide glue. Fresh, commercial water-soluble block-out can also be used.

Silk serves best as the screen fabric because of its greater porosity, but multifilament dacron can be used with satisfactory results. Meshes coarser than 12xx should be avoided, since the increased

7.1 A print made from a resist stencil in which drawing and rubbing with litho crayon and liquid frisket were used.

space between threads requires a coat of glue so thick that fine detail cannot be held or recorded.

POSITIVE DRAWING

Although you can draw on the screen with crayon and tusche by working from a drawing or sketch, this stencil technique is most suited to the development of an idea as you go. Many interesting effects that are

7.2 Examples of a variety of materials used in different ways to make a resist stencil. From top: lithographic crayon, ordinary crayon, oil pastel, lithographic tusche used with pen and brush and stamped, latex liquid frisket used with pen and brush, hide glue used with pen, brush, and stamping, and dry-transfer materials applied directly to the screen.

difficult to obtain by drawing alone can be obtained with the resist stencil.

The quality of a line drawn with a litho crayon will vary greatly depending on the texture of the surface beneath the screen. And any number of different textured or relief objects may be placed beneath the screen and rubbings taken of them with the litho crayon. In fact, the effects obtainable are limitless.

When drawing directly with crayon or oil pastels, always make the image somewhat darker than you want it in your print. Fine grays tend to disappear when the screen is glued in. To get an idea of how the print will look, hold the screen to a bright white wall or window. Strong diffused light will tend to eliminate the lighter grays and show what will appear in the print.

When using tusche or toosh, put it down opaquely. This ensures that the fabric is completely sealed from the glue.

When fine, sharp lines are needed, use the latex liquid frisket in a lettering pen.

Once the drawing is completed, dust the

screen with talcum powder and tap the excess talc out of the screen. The powder helps to harden litho crayon and make it resistant to streaking or smearing. It also increases the incompatibility of the drawn areas and the glue block-out.

Always mix your glue (1 part water and 1 part glue) fresh. (It tends to spoil rapidly.) With the screen elevated so that it is level but not in contact with the surface below, pour a small puddle of glue into the well or tape mask of the screen. With a piece of cardboard measuring about 2" x 3", spread the glue in a zigzag, snowplow fashion over the screen, pushing the bead of glue ahead to where the next pass will be (Figure 7.3). Scrape off any drips or beads immediately for they may affect the printed image.

7.3 Gluing in the screen. Note the angle at which the cardboard is held as it moves across the screen.

Allow this coat to dry thoroughly. Repeat the application and again allow it to dry. Inspect the stencil for pinholes and evenness of the coating. If the glue is fresh, the applications uniform, and the screen clean, two coats will suffice. If there are many pinholes after the second coat, a third coat must be applied. But avoid more than three, as the glue build-up on the drawing becomes difficult to remove when you go to clear the stencil.

When applying commercial water-soluble

block-outs, work very rapidly, and do not go back over the drawn areas. The solvent in the block-outs attacks crayon and tusche and can cause it to streak and smear.

To remove the crayon and tusche before printing, place a pad of newspaper beneath the screen and sprinkle turpentine on it. Lower the screen onto the paper and sprinkle more turpentine on the screen (Figure 7.4). Allow it to stand for a few seconds. Lift the screen, and using a brass suede brush, scrub the underside of the screen gently to loosen the crayon and tusche. As they are dissolved, any glue on top will flake away easily.

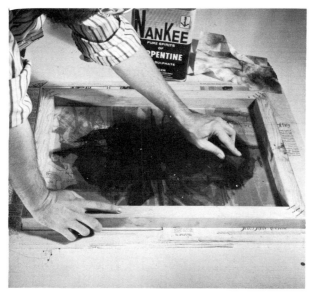

7.5   Scrubbing from the inside of the screen.

brushes to avoid tearing the silk. Generally, the brushes should be used sparingly, and then with as little pressure as possible, especially with thin glue, or pinholes may develop.

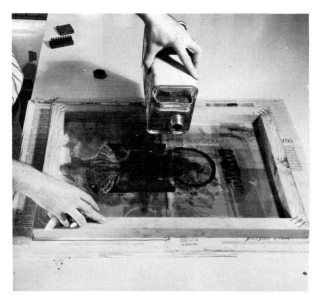

7.4   After the glue is dry, screen is lowered onto a pad of newspaper and turpentine is sprinkled on.

Now lower the screen and scrub it gently from the top (Figure 7.5). With paper toweling, mop up the dissolved crayon, tusche, and loose glue and peel off the saturated layer of newspaper (Figure 7.6). Continue working in this manner until most of the drawing is gone. Where the crayon was applied lightly or where dry brush effects were employed, you will probably still see deposits sealed in glue. Concentrate your scrubbing where there are clearly heavy deposits of crayon or tusche. For particularly stubborn areas two brushes can be used simultaneously, one on each side of the screen. Be careful to scrub in the same direction with both

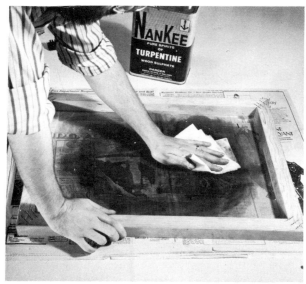

7.6   Mopping up dissolved crayon and tusche.

An alternative to brushing is to use a dull palette knife to scrape the surface of the stencil lightly, causing the glue on the crayon to flake off.

If latex or rubber cement has been used, remove it before removing the crayon with a wad of rubber cement or a rubber cement pick-up (Figure 7.7).

7.7   Removing latex liquid frisket with a rubber cement pick-up.

To determine whether a screen is clear, dry it and hold it up to a strong, indirect light source and scan the stencil. The printing areas will pass light freely, allowing you to see through the screen. The glue-resist areas will be only translucent. Pinholes will appear as bright pinpoints of light.

When the screen is 90 percent clear of the original drawing, corrections can be made with the glue. After making sure that the screen is completely dry, paint out any unwanted open areas or pinholes with the same glue solution. When these corrections are dry, you are ready to print.

Since the glue is water-soluble, it is very easy to remove the stencil after printing is completed. Easiest is to take the screen into a shower and wash it thoroughly with hot water. If this is not possible, place a large pad of newspaper on the worktable and soak it with water. Lower the screen onto the pad and add more water. Place a pad of paper on the screen, add more water, and soak thoroughly (Figure 7.8).

Allow the screen to sit for about a half hour and discard the paper. Scrub the screen with clean toweling and warm water

7.8a   Pouring water onto a pad of newspaper beneath the screen.

7.8b   Screen lowered and more water being added.

7.8c   Paper being placed on top of screen and more water being added.

until any moisture picked up from the screen no longer feels sticky when tightly pressed between thumb and forefinger.

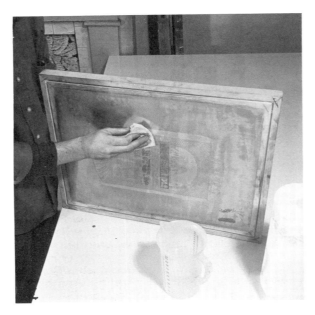

7.8d After soaking off most of the glue, the screen is scrubbed with wet paper toweling to remove remaining traces of glue.

Since some crayon or tusche may have been sealed in the glue, scrubbing with lacquer thinner as a final step may be necessary to complete clean-up.

NEGATIVE DRAWING

It is possible to work directly with the glue in forming the stencil. It can be painted with brushes, used in lettering pens, or sprayed with an airbrush. It can also be applied to textured surfaces or objects that are pressed onto the screen. India ink is frequently added to the glue to make it more visible.

When working directly with the glue, you may find it necessary to alter its consistency. For painting with a brush, a solution of equal parts of glue and water works well, but when using a pen, the glue may have to be thinned. When coating surfaces to be pressed into the screen, you may use the glue undiluted.

Although one can use commercial water-soluble block-outs for direct work, they dry rapidly and so tend to clog pens and brushes. Rapid drying, however, is one advantage of such materials: their use decreases the waiting time between steps. And because the water-soluble block-outs have superior surface tension (compared with glue), very frequently only one coat will be necessary. This is particularly true

when the block-out is fresh and is used with fabrics finer than 12xx.

As previously mentioned, it is particularly important that the water-soluble block-out be completely dry before attempting to remove the crayon or tusche.

When working with resist methods, always apply both the drawing and the block-out stencil material to the same side of the screen. Otherwise the drawing will not adequately protect the fabric from the stencil, which will be on one side and the drawing on the other. Although, as a rule, the drawing and the stencil material are applied to the squeegee side of the screen, printing will go equally well if both are applied to the printing side.

Dry-transfer photomechanical aids such as Lettraset, Prestype, and so on can be applied directly to the screen as part of your drawing. They effectively seal the fabric from the glue or block-out and are easily removed with turpentine.

PROGRESSIVE BLOCK-OUT

All stencil techniques can be used to progressively block out a stencil for multicolor printing. Resist stencils are most frequently used in this way since it is relatively easy to paint out areas with the glue and reprint the stencil in another color.

Drawing and rubbing with the crayon can also be done progressively in the open areas of the screen, gluing in the screen in the normal manner. When working this way, remember that only where crayon is put down in the remaining open areas of the original stencil will it print the next time. This can be repeated as often as desired, or as open areas permit.

COMBINED STENCILS

Many different stencil materials can be combined because their individual natures are unaffected by each other's solvent. Lacquer and resist, water-soluble knife-cut and lacquer knife-cut, and certain indirect photo stencils and lacquer stencils may be combined for various purposes and effects (Figure 7.9).

Sometimes stencils are combined to achieve certain effects in one printing that would be difficult to achieve with a single stencil technique. Other times this is done to modify a stencil for successive printings in different colors.

7.9 An example in which several stencils were combined at various stages of the printing.

LACQUER KNIFE-CUT AND GLUE-RESIST STENCILS

There are three different ways to use lacquer and glue-resist stencils together. A lacquer stencil can be adhered to the screen and then a resist stencil drawn in the open portions of the lacquer stencil (Figure 7.10). They are then printed as one.

7.10 Applying crayon texture to open areas of lacquer stencil.

The second way begins as before, but after the combined stencil has been printed, the glue is removed and the lacquer stencil is printed alone over the first printing with a transparent color. Since nothing has changed, the registration of the second printing can be extremely accurate.

In the third way the lacquer stencil is printed alone first, and then the resist stencil is added to the open portions of the lacquer stencil, and they are printed together a second time either transparently or opaquely.

The application of resist stencil materials has no effect on the lacquer. However, if the lacquer stencil is to be removed instead of the glue, some breakdown of the glue may occur from the lacquer thinner. Caution should be observed when scrubbing out the crayon to prevent abrading the edges of the lacquer stencil. Removal of the glue will have no effect on the lacquer stencil.

LACQUER KNIFE-CUT AND WATER-SOLUBLE KNIFE-CUT STENCILS

Since the image quality of these two stencils is the same, they are generally used together where it is necessary to add or to remove shapes of a similar kind without affecting the remaining portions of the stencil.

The lacquer stencil is always adhered first. After it is printed, the water-soluble stencil is added to the open areas of the lacquer, and together they are printed in a second color over the first (Figure 7.11).

7.11 Adhering a knife-cut water-soluble stencil to an open area of a lacquer stencil.

In a second procedure both a lacquer stencil and a water-soluble stencil are adhered, and they are printed together for the first color. The water-soluble stencil is then removed, and a second color is printed transparently over the first.

LACQUER KNIFE-CUT AND INDIRECT PHOTO STENCILS

Like the other combinations, these two work well because they are unaffected by each other's solvents. Which is adhered first depends on which is to be removed before printing the second color, or which is going to be added for the second color (Figure 7.12).

The direct photo stencil emulsions do not work as reliably. Because they are mildly affected by lacquer thinner, they may break down if the lacquer stencil is applied over the direct emulsion or if it is removed before the direct emulsion.

PRINTED POSITIVES

Under some circumstances it is not possible to combine the different stencil techniques. The two techniques may require similar solvents, and removal or adhesion of one stencil may destroy the other. If, for instance, one desires to combine the textural effects of a resist stencil with a photo image on a photo stencil, the first stencil may be damaged in the preparation of the second.

7.12 Preparing to adhere a photo stencil to an open area of a lacquer stencil. A previously adhered water-soluble stencil has been peeled off.

One way around this difficulty is to prepare the resist stencil separately and print it in opaque black ink on acetate. The photo positive for the photo image can then be taped to the acetate in the proper position and together they can be used to make the photo stencil.

8. printing

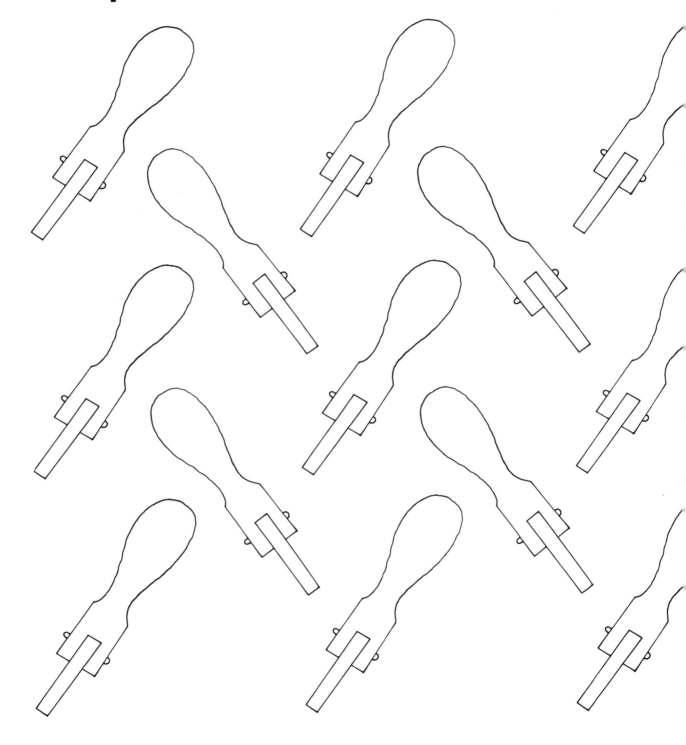

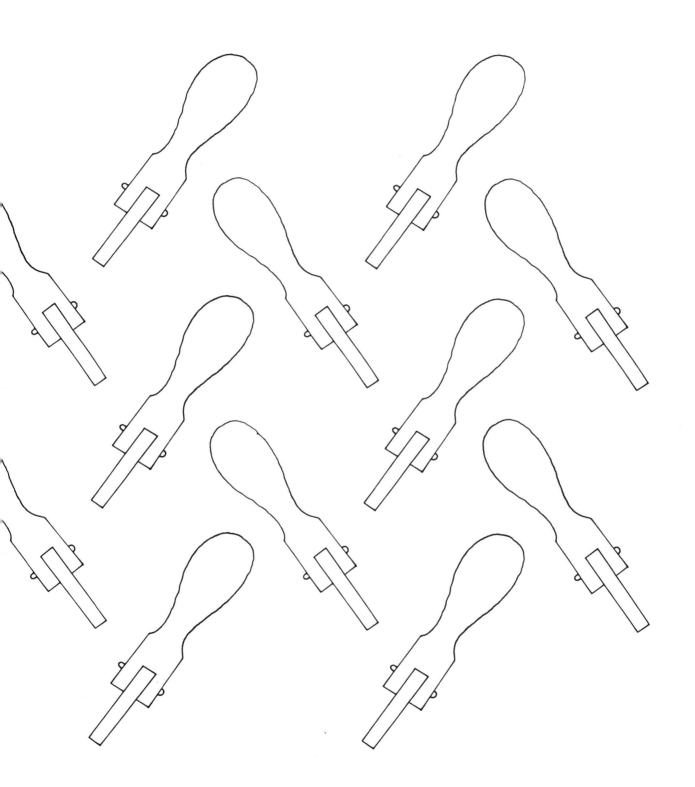

The artist begins with an idea, and to achieve that idea he makes many decisions about the techniques and materials of his art. The realization of the idea (or the failure to realize it) becomes manifest at the end of the printing phase of silk-screening. If the idea has been good, and the techniques used equally good, the print will be good. But if the idea has been weak or poor, a mastery of technique will not suffice; technique alone will not compensate for a poor idea.

Everything comes together, then, at the printing stage. The print is the goal. Tools, equipment, materials, inks, solvents, block-outs, and stencils are but means to this end. All that remains, finally, is to print. If all has gone well, you will have all the following items ready:

1. A screen with a tightly stretched, well-prepared fabric in good condition.

2. A stencil adhered to the screen, with unwanted areas blocked out.

3. A system for hinging the screen to a smooth printing surface.

4. A well-sharpened squeegee of the appropriate length and hardness.

5. Ink, in sufficient quantity, properly prepared for printing.

6. Printing paper cut to size.

7. Registration tabs for the printing paper.

8. A drying rack or place to dry the prints.

9. Solvents and thinners for thinning the ink and for cleaning up after printing.

10. Paper toweling for clean-up and for wiping up spills.

11. A palette knife or spatula for mixing and scooping up ink.

12. Masking tape, for emergency block-out repairs.

13. A hatpin to remove clogged pinholes or dust.

14. A garbage can.

THE PRINTING PROCESS

The sequence of the actual steps in printing follows.

1. Place the paper in registration tabs.

2. Lower the screen.

3. Pour or scoop the ink into screen well at back.

4. Place the squeegee behind the ink and pull it forward.

5. Lift the squeegee and return it to the far end of the screen.

6. Raise and support the screen.

7. Remove the print to drying area.

8. Examine the print for imperfections and take corrective steps as needed.

9. Place a new piece of paper in registration tabs.

10. Lower the screen.

11. Bring the squeegee to the front of the screen and push it to the back.

12. Raise and support the screen.

13. Remove the print to the drying area.

14. Examine the print for imperfections and take corrective steps as needed.

15. Repeat the above steps until all prints are finished.

16. Add fresh ink periodically, as needed.

17. Thoroughly remove all traces of ink from the screen when printing is completed.

18. Remove the stencil from the screen (if of the solvent-adhering type).

PAPER

Although paper is the most common material used by the artist, and is the cheapest and most readily available, any reasonably flat material can be printed upon. (For a discussion of other materials, see Chapter 2 and Appendix 2.)

Any paper can be printed with ordinary process-type poster inks (ethyl cellulose), including metallic papers, clay-coated papers, chrome-coated papers, flocked papers, tracing paper, and newsprint.

The paper may have a smooth finish, or it may have a heavy tooth, or calender. It may be lightweight paper or heavy cardboard. Although, generally, fairly smooth papers are used by the artist, interesting textural effects can be obtained when thin, transparent colors are printed on heavily textured papers.

The artist is advised to cut all printing paper to the same size, and the chosen size should be one that can be contained on the printing surface.

PAPER REGISTRATION

In many instances the registration tabs for the printing paper will be established before a stencil is adhered to the screen. For one-color work, or for the first stencil in multi-color printing, you may set the tabs just before printing. (See p. 59 for discussion of tabs.)

PAPER REGISTRATION FOR ODD-SIZED OR ODD-EDGED PAPER

On occasion in multicolor printing you may wish to print the same stencil on a variety of stocks and sizes of paper, or you may have selected a paper with a very pronounced and soft deckle edge. Here registration tabs will be unreliable, and a system allowing accurate visual placement must be used.

A sheet of clear, 5-mil acetate is taped along one side on the printing surface under the screen (Figure 8.1). The sheet should be sufficiently large to accommodate the largest sheet of printing paper you wish to use.

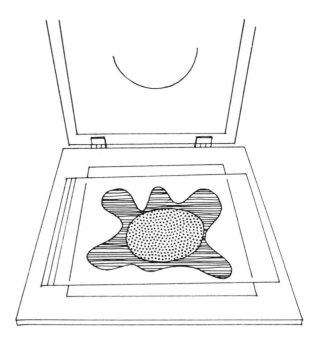

8.2   Image of second color printed onto acetate.

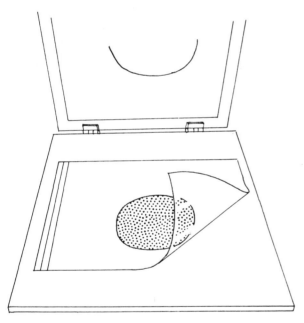

8.1   A sheet of thin acetate taped at one side beneath the screen.

The screen is lowered and the first impression of the second color is printed directly onto the acetate and allowed to dry (Figure 8.2). Then a copy of the first color print is slipped under the acetate and positioned in accurate register to the second color on the acetate.

The acetate is then gently lifted out of the way without disturbing the position of the paper, and the second color is printed accurately in register on the first (Figure 8.3).

This is a more time-consuming method than using mechanical tabs, and considerably more care must be exercised to prevent prints from shifting out of register.

POSITIONING THE PAPER FOR PRINTING

The paper is positioned so that it fits snugly and still lies flat (Figure 8.4). Time will be saved if you learn to sense how the paper feels when properly positioned by tugging gently at the corner between the two registration sides. But until you are sure of the feel of the fit, check the positioning visually.

LOWERING THE SCREEN

Remove the screen support and lower the screen slowly on to the printing surface. Do not let it slam down: the downdraft can throw the paper out of register.

POURING INK INTO THE SCREEN WELL

Place enough ink for several prints in the nonprinting area at the far end of the screen (Figure 8.5), and distribute it across the width of the print. Do not pour the ink directly onto any portion of the stencil,

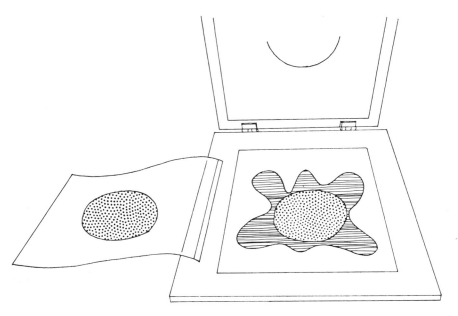

8.3 The acetate is lifted out of the way, and the second color is printed accurately onto the first.

8.4 Positioning printing paper in registration tabs.

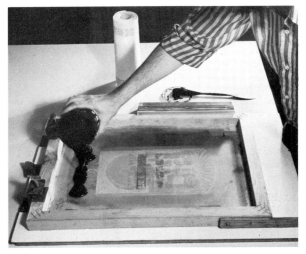

8.5 Pouring bead of ink into well of screen.

as then the weight of the ink will cause it to drip through and ruin the print. Remember, too, that it is always better to have too much ink in the screen than too little.

POSITIONING THE SQUEEGEE AND PRINTING

Position the squeegee behind the ink and lean it toward you at about a 60-degree angle. Using both hands, pull the squeegee toward you, exerting uniform pressure so that you can hear the fabric whistle as you pull (Figure 8.6). Do not press down so hard that the squeegee blade bends down flat on to the screen. Pull the squeegee smoothly and continuously. Do not stop your motion until you have passed completely over the printing areas. If you should stop or change the pressure or speed up, unwanted lines or uneven ink deposits will appear, especially in broad areas of color.

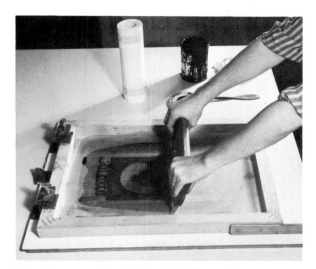

8.6   Squeegee in middle of printing stroke.

SQUEEGEE RETURN

At the end of the first printing stroke, temporarily return the squeegee to the far end of the screen while removing the print and placing fresh paper in the tabs. To do this, pull the squeegee as far forward as possible, and then back it off a couple of inches, essentially wiping off the excess ink. Do not back the squeegee on to the printing area. If there is insufficient room to avoid this, raise one end of the squeegee up at the end of the printing stroke so that the excess ink can flow down the squeegee into the well (Figure 8.7). Then return the squeegee to the far end of the screen and prop it upright against the frame.

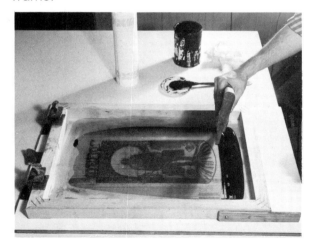

8.7   Lifting squeegee at one end to allow excess ink to drip off into well.

RAISING THE SCREEN

Raise the screen and support it on its leg. If the ink is properly mixed, the print should not stick to the screen (Figure 8.8). If the print does stick, or hesitates in its release, peel it off slowly and uniformly. Do not slide it off; that can cause blurring of edges. Raising the screen with a snap can help effect good, instantaneous release of the print, but this should not be done with paper stencils—they may be pulled off the screen along with the print.

8.8   Squeegee propped at back of screen, screen elevated by a leg and the print being removed.

DRYING THE PRINT

Remove the print to the drying area. Most process-type inks dry in fifteen to thirty minutes. They dry faster when the print is hanging than when lying flat.

EXAMINING THE PRINT

The first few prints need to be examined for flaws and imperfections, either in the stencil or in the printing process. The first few may have a slightly weak appearance until the ink has had a chance to thoroughly saturate the fabric. Take such corrective measures as are necessary to eliminate any problems. (Various problems and their in-printing solutions are discussed in "Problems and Solutions"—pp. 128 to 138.)

THE SECOND PRINT

Place a new piece of paper in the tabs and lower the screen. Now, since the bulk of the ink is at the front of the screen, the squeegee stroke will be from front to back. There are three ways to do this. You can bring the squeegee forward and lean it **away** from you at an angle of about 60 degrees and push it firmly and steadily to the back, where you will again rest it against the frame (Figure 8.9).

8.9   Leaning squeegee away and pushing to far side for second print.

A better way is to lean the squeegee **toward** you at a 60-degree angle and push it to the back of the screen (Figure 8.10). This works well with the neoprene squeegees, but many of the plastic blades tend to bind and skip when used in this fashion. Also, if the blade or handle is warped or not true, maintaining a smooth stroke and uniform pressure may be difficult.

8.10   Leaning squeegee toward you and pushing to far side for second print.

Some people, finding it difficult to maintain constant pressure, prefer to walk around the table and pull the squeegee toward them. This obviously works, and is fine if you like exercise, but it eats up time. And it is practicable only if the worktable is away from a wall.

From this point, the printing procedure is simply repeated, except that ink is added as needed. Although you will want sufficient ink in the screen at the beginning for about ten prints, you will not want more. Beyond this, printing becomes messy, and the ink tends to stiffen up. It is better to add ink every five prints or so to maintain the ink in the screen at the proper consistency.

CLEAN-UP

An important, if unpleasant, part of the printing procedure is the cleaning up afterward. Too often artists create problems for themselves by glossing over it. To this point you may not have gotten a speck of ink on you, but from here on it is messy work. Unless you wear gloves, it is impossible to keep your hands clean during clean-up. The procedure that follows is, if not the neatest, one of the quickest and easiest, and it requires a minimum of solvent.

Spread a pad of opened newspaper under the screen. Strip away any paper or masking tape from the screen. Lower the screen and scoop out as much excess ink as possible with a palette knife or spatula and return it to the ink container (Figure 8.11). Scrape all ink off the squeegee

8.11   Scooping up excess ink at the end of printing.

(Figure 8.12). Take the squeegee and make several passes across the screen as if printing (Figure 8.13). Lift the screen and discard the top sheet of newspaper.

Lower the screen and sprinkle turpentine over the entire screen. With folded paper toweling, mop the screen until the toweling is completely saturated with ink (Figure 8.14). Discard the towel. Raise the screen and discard the top sheet of newspaper (Figure 8.15). Repeat this process twice more.

8.14 Scrubbing and mopping turpentine-dissolved ink.

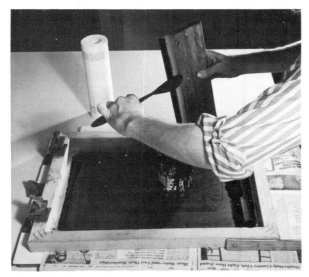

8.12 Scraping excess ink off squeegee.

8.15 Top sheet of saturated newspaper being removed.

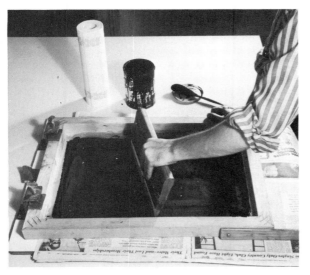

8.13 Printing out ink residue onto newsprint to make clean-up easier.

At this point, virtually all ink should be removed from the screen, and all that remains should appear to be an ink stain. With the screen in a vertical position, scrub from both sides with two pads of paper toweling saturated with turpentine (Figure 8.16). Continually refold or replace and saturate the toweling with turpentine as needed. Work in this way until the towels fail to pick up any traces of ink and the screen is free of all but the faintest ink stain. Thoroughly dry the screen with clean, dry toweling. It may now be stored for future printings or it may be reclaimed.

8.16   Scrubbing the screen from both sides as final clean-up.

RECLAIMING THE SCREEN

If you do not plan to use the stencil again, you are well advised to remove it as soon as possible. Most stencils harden with age and require much more work to remove later on. A good habit is to remove the stencil as yet another step in the clean-up. For specific instructions on removing various block-outs and stencils, see the chapters where they are discussed. In general, use the following procedure in the recovery of a screen, regardless of the fabric or stencil or block-out.

1. Remove all tape and paper from the screen.

2. Clean ink thoroughly from the screen and dry it.

3. Use cold water to remove any block-outs that require it.

4. Use hot water to remove block-outs on stencils that permit it.

5. Follow the necessary steps for removing the stencil.

6. Inspect the screen for clogged areas and use the appropriate solvent to clear them.

This sequence is important—not just for expediency but also to minimize problems that may emerge from the incompatibility of certain stencil and block-out solvents. A review of some of the materials used in screen recovery and their problems follows.

Cold Water: This is used to remove many kinds of water-soluble block-outs and will remove some water-soluble knife-cut stencils and hide glue. It does not harm materials that require hot water, lacquer thinner, or enzymes.
Hot Water: Hot water follows cold when removing water-soluble block-outs because hot water renders many of them insoluble in water. Many types of photo stencils are removed with hot water, and hide glue and water-soluble knife-cut stencils are removed more easily with it.
Lacquer Thinner: Water is used to remove block-outs before a lacquer stencil is removed, since lacquer thinner may amalgamate with the block-out. Removing the block-out first also makes for more complete removal of the stencil, since the block-out was applied over the stencil.

VARIATIONS IN THE PRINTING PROCESS

The process of printing is clearly not overly complicated: you have covered the basics. You should, however, also know certain variations, since you may need them at any time to solve problems that emerge during printing.

CONTACT PRINTING

Contact printing means that the screen is in tight contact with the printing stock at all times. This method should be used with small screens under 18″ x 24″. Many people prefer it even with larger screens because the pressure of the screen helps to hold the paper in place. When printing thin or flimsy material, contact printing is often the best method if you do not have a vacuum printing table. And if you use paper stencils, it must be employed in order to keep the stencil properly attached and in register and to prevent buckling of the stencil.

Contact printing does have disadvantages. If the screen fabric is at all slack, the edges of shapes are likely to blur because the silk shifts when the squeegee is pulled across it.

The screen frame must be free of warp, and the printing surface must be flat, to prevent uneven ink deposits. In fact, because of the tight contact, the squeegee does not push ink all the way through the screen. Not until the screen is lifted and separated from the print does the ink pass completely through. As a result, a considerable residue is left among the fibers of the screen, and this tends to stiffen and clog the screen. There is also a greater tendency for the prints to stick to the screen when it is raised.

OFF-CONTACT PRINTING

In off-contact printing the screen is elevated a uniform distance above the printing surface, usually between ⅛ and ¼ inch (Figure 8.17). The pressure of the squeegee stroke forces the screen fabric down on to the print only along the line where the squeegee touches (Figure 8.18). The screen separates from the print immediately after the squeegee passes, ensuring

8.17   Comparing contact and off-contact printing arrangements. Ordinary butt hinges can be used for off-contact printing merely by shimming them off the printing surface.

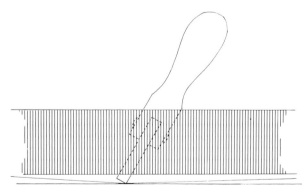

8.18   The screen fabric touches the printing surface only at the point where the squeegee passes, effecting instantaneous release of the print from the screen.

complete passage of the ink through the screen and resulting in less clogging.

Fine details and sharp edges are easier to maintain with off-contact printing because any shift in the fabric during the squeegee stroke does not blur the edges. Off-contact printing permits visual inspection of print registration through the stencil with the screen in printing position. And since absolute uniformity of the distance between printing surface and screen is not critical, some warp in the screen frame or printing surface will not have a detrimental effect.

This method is particularly well suited to the printing of large, broad areas of color, since the instant release of the screen from the paper ensures uniform and blemish-free printing.

One disadvantage is that it is almost impossible to print with a multiple squeegee stroke (see p. 128) without blurring edges—the screen fabric stretches during printing. This stretching can also cause distortion or displacement of the stencil, occasionally causing misregistration. Thus it is sometimes necessary to allow more overlap in stencils that abut one another to compensate for this.

In off-contact printing, it is almost mandatory that the squeegee be pulled in the same direction every time, unless sufficient overlap is provided for in the stencils. Sometimes it is necessary to compensate for the shift by deliberately misregistering the stencils during adhesion.

Paper stencils cannot be printed off-contact because the shifting fabric causes the stencil to creep or buckle, with the possibility of ink squirting under the stencil.

Finally, off-contact printing works best on large screens where the squeegee is less than two-thirds the width of the screen.

FLOOD STROKE

By drawing the squeegee and ink across the screen without the squeegee coming in contact with the printing surface below, the stencil becomes flooded with ink (Figure 8.19). The purpose of this is to rewet and unclog ink or to prevent clogging of fine detail.

Although many artists rarely if ever employ the flood stroke, there are times when its use has great advantages. These are:

1.   when there is going to be a delay in

8.19 Elevated screen being flooded with ink.

The usual reason for wanting to make a second pass with the squeegee is the knowledge or expectation that one stroke did not make a perfect impression. Reject the poor print and take other corrective measures to improve the quality of future prints.

The main reason for using a multiple stroke is when a thicker ink deposit is desired, but even here it is generally better to use a flood stroke to achieve this if it is not possible to do so through ink modification or squeegee selection.

Many problems arise from using a multiple stroke. These are:

1.   noticeably uneven ink deposit on print caused by differences in ink flow with each stroke;

2.   blurring of the edges of shapes caused by slight shift in paper, screen frame, or fabric;

3.   loss of fine detail;

4.   ink squirting under the stencil;

5.   a noticeable texture to the ink;

6.   rewetting and mixing with previously printed colors;

7.   offsetting of the first stroke image onto the underside of the stencil, causing a ghost to appear on the next print;

8.   loss of transparency when using transparent colors.

the middle of printing and you do not want to clean up your screen;

2.   when fine detail tends to become blocked or plugged up during printing, from rapid drying, ink that is too heavy, or tackiness of ink;

3.   when printing on 16xx meshes or finer;

4.   when it is a more convenient way to get ink from the near to far end of the screen to permit printing in the same direction for all prints;

5.   when printing images larger than 18" x 24" or broad areas of color;

6.   when a heavier ink deposit is desired without having to change squeegees, to change ink consistency;

7.   when printing tacky materials such as plastic inks, lacquers, or varnishes.

You may choose to use a flood stroke after every print or after every three or four prints or only when a problem occurs. Generally, when printing editions of more than thirty, it is a good idea to intersperse a flood stroke at regular intervals to ensure uniformity of the print quality throughout the edition.

MULTIPLE STROKE

There may be times when you feel it necessary to use a second pass with the squeegee in order to get a good print of the stencil. Resist the temptation! Nine times out of ten the second stroke will do no good.

PROBLEMS AND SOLUTIONS

It is one thing to follow a prescribed procedure and quite another when something goes wrong. One is less likely to encounter problems during printing if good and consistent work habits are developed.

The most common source of trouble in printing is the squeegee, its condition, care, and use. And, for the most part, the printing problems that arise can be divided into three categories: (1) Less ink is being printed than is desired. (2) More ink is being printed than is desired. (3) The printed ink is not positioned properly. Essentially, these are cases of "too little," "too much," and "in the wrong place."

TROUBLESHOOTING

The biggest problem is knowing where to look for the causes. In the case of "too little," any of the following may contribute:

1. The condition and application of the squeegee.
2. The condition of the screen.
3. The consistency of the ink.

In the case of "too much," these factors may also contribute:

1. The condition of the block-out.
2. The condition of the stencil.

In the case of "the wrong place," the following may be additional contributing factors:

1. Paper misregistration.
2. Stencil misregistration.
3. Loose screen hinges.
4. Off-contact printing.

The following are the more common printing problems, their causes, in-printing solutions (where possible), and the preventions.

1. The edges of shapes do not print clearly (Figure 8.20).

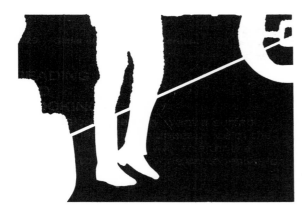

8.20   Upper half shows blurred edges of shapes.

Causes:
    A. Dull squeegee.
    B. Thick stencil.
    C. Hard squeegee used on coarse printing paper.
    D. Soft squeegee used on smooth paper.
    E. Thick ink.
    F. Uneven printing surface.
    G. Fast-drying ink.
    H. Delay between prints.

Solutions:
    A. Sharpen the squeegee.
    B. None, if E, G, and H below do not work.
    C. and D. Change to an appropriate squeegee.
    E. Remove ink from screen and thin it.
    F. Increase squeegee pressure, employ a flood stroke, use a softer squeegee, or switch to a different printing surface.
    G. and H. Employ a flood stroke with each impression.

Preventions:
    A. Thoroughly sharpen squeegee before printing.
    B. Recut stencil on thinner material or expose or adhere to produce thinner stencils.
    C. and D. See Solutions C and D.
    E. Mix ink to the proper consistency before printing.
    F. Establish a smooth, flat printing surface before printing.
    G. and H. When mixing ink, use a retarder thinner.

2. The edges of shapes have a saw-tooth appearance.

Causes:
    A. Ink too thick.
    B. Stencil melted during adhesion.
    C. Old multifilament fabric.
    D. Improper amounts of transparent base.
    E. Dull squeegee.
    F. Squeegee too soft.
    G. Thick stencil.
    H. Fabric mesh too coarse.

Solutions:
    A. Remove ink from screen and thin it.
    B. None.

C. None, if following solutions do not work.
D. Add transparent base, but keep the ink fluid.
E. Flood screen, and clean and sharpen squeegee.
F. Use a harder squeegee.
G. and H. None, if above solutions do not work.

Preventions: A. D. E. F. See Solutions.
B. Recut and adhere stencil correctly.
C. Clean screen thoroughly and re-stretch when badly clogged.
G. Recut thinner paper stencils, recut and adhere solvent-type stencils to produce thinner stencil. Re-expose photo stencils to produce thinner stencils.
H. For fine detail, use only 12xx or finer meshes, or the equivalents.

3. White spots appear in the solid areas of color.

Causes: A. Dust picked up by the screen.
B. Ink particles left in the screen from previous printing.
C. Particles of stencil or block-out left from previous printing.

Solutions: A. Use fingernail or dull palette knife to flick off the dust from underside.
B. and C. Use a hat-pin and poke between the fibers from the inside of the screen. If this does not loosen the particles, clean the area with ink solvent and use the appropriate solvent to remove the spots.

Preventions: A. Make sure the screen and printing surface are dust-free before printing.
B. and C. Check the screen thoroughly against a strong indirect light to detect any pinhole blocks. Remove with appropriate solvent.

4. The print sticks to the screen after printing.

Causes: A. Insufficient transparent base in the ink.
B. Ink is too stiff.
C. Dull squeegee.
D. Static electricity.
E. Insufficient squeegee pressure during printing.
F. Contact printing.

Solutions: A. Remove ink and add transparent base to it.
B. Remove ink and thin it.
C. Sharpen the squeegee.
D. When raising the screen, snap it up rapidly.
E. Increase squeegee pressure.
F. Raise screen immediately after printing stroke.

Preventions: A. through C. Follow Solutions A, B, and C.
D. See Solution D.
E. Apply greater squeegee pressure during printing.
F. Print off-contact whenever possible.

5. The ink squirts under the edges of the stencil.

Causes: A. Slack screen.
B. Thick stencil.
C. Poorly attached paper stencil.

D. Dull squeegee.
E. Soft squeegee.
F. Thin ink.

Solutions: A. and B. Reduce squeegee pressure.
C. Detach tape and stretch stencil out smoothly.
D. Sharpen the squeegee.
E. Use a harder squeegee.
F. Remove ink and add transparent base to it.

Preventions: A. Check screen for tautness before attaching stencils. Restretch screen as needed.
B. If a paper stencil, print onto thinner stencil paper and recut. If a lacquer stencil, recut and adhere for minimum thickness. If a photo stencil, re-expose at reduced exposure time to produce thinner stencil.
C. through F. Follow Solutions C through F as normal preventive measures.

6. Hairline streaks of ink appear along the edges of printed shapes, usually near the top. They are not always exactly the same, nor in the same place.

Causes: A. Uneven release of the print from the screen.
B. Paper shifting after printing while still in contact with screen.

Solutions: A. and B. Add more transparent base and thinner (if ink is too thick). Make sure that the print falls away from the screen rather than sliding off it. Use a flood stroke or print off-contact when possible. See Problem 4 for causes and solutions relating to prints sticking.

7. Large solid areas of color do not print uniformly. The color in certain areas appears thinner or weaker than in other areas (Figure 8.21).

Causes: A. Warped squeegee.
B. Uneven printing surface.
C. Warped screen frame.
D. Uneven squeegee pressure.
E. Thick ink.
F. Clogged screen fabric.

Solutions: A. Change squeegee.
B. Change the printing surface or use a softer squeegee.
C. Switch to off-contact printing.
D. Use proper squeegee angle and constant, uniform pressure.
E. Remove ink and thin it.
F. Employ a flood stroke.

Preventions: A. Replace warped squeegee handle. Maintain squeegee blade in good, straight condition through correct sharpening.
B. When printing large solid areas of color, make sure printing surface is as flat as possible.
C. Plan to print broad areas of color in off-contact to minimize the problems encountered with warped screens.
D. and E. Follow Solutions D and E as normal preventive measures.
F. Check screen and clean it thoroughly before use. Replace as needed.

8.21   Uneven ink deposit.

8.   A darker line of the same color as printed appears in solid areas.

Causes: A.   Nicked squeegee blade.
               B.   Run in screen fabric.

Solutions: A.   Clean and sharpen squeegee until nick disappears.
               B.   None.

Preventions: A.   See Solution A.
               B.   Examine the screen for runs and replace it if necessary.

9.   A line or shape appears to print slightly weaker or lighter in a solid area of color, yet there is no apparent clogging of the screen.

Causes: A.   Old multifilament fabric that was used for a long printing run.
               B.   Old multifilament fabric on which a stencil was left for a long time.
               C.   Multifilament fabric that had ink residue left in it for a long time.
               D.   A piece of paper or tape on the printing surface.

Solutions: A. through C. None.
               D.   Check printing sur-

face for tape or other bumps.

Preventions: A. through C. Clean the screen thoroughly with volatile solvent such as acetone or ethylene dichloride. Replace the screen if necessary.
               D.   Clean the printing surface thoroughly before printing.

10.   Different areas of the same color have differing degrees of opacity.

Cause: The use of a multiple stroke to print image completely.

Solution: None.

Prevention: Maintain sufficient ink in screen to print image completely with one pass of the squeegee.

11.   Darker spots of the same color appear in solid areas.

Cause: Ink dripping onto printing areas.

Solution: None; self-clearing with next impression.

Prevention: Make sure that no ink drips onto the stencil when the squeegee is moved to the back of the screen.

12.   A pockmarked effect appears in a linear pattern but not always in the same place.

Causes: The print sticks to the screen or hesitates in its release. See Problems 4 and 6 for details, Solutions, and Preventions.

13.   The printed ink shows the texture of the screen fabric.

Causes: A.   Thick ink.
               B.   Too much transparent base.
               C.   Soft squeegee.
               D.   Dull squeegee.

Solutions: A.   Remove the ink and add appropriate thinner to it.
               B.   Remove the ink and remix it with

less transparent
base.
C. Use a harder
squeegee.
D. Sharpen the
squeegee.

Preventions: A. through D. Follow
Solutions A through
D as normal pre-
ventive measures.

14. Transparent colors show signs of a
texture or pattern that is not in the stencil.

Causes: A. Screen fabric too
coarse.
B. Rough or textured
printing surface.
C. Heavily textured
printing paper.
D. Transparent base
only used to reduce
the inks.

Solutions: A. None.
B. Change to a
smooth printing
surface.
C. Print on a smooth
paper.
D. None.

Preventions: A. Use 12xx or
finer fabrics.
B. and C. See
Solutions B and C.
D. Use a toner or
crystal clear base
in addition to the
transparent base.

15. A noticeable line appears where
two colors overlap.

Causes: A. Light color printed
over dark one.
B. Transparent ink.
C. First color not dry
before printing
second.
D. First color printed
too thickly.
E. Second color
printed with
multiple strokes.

Solutions: A. Use a minimum
transparent base
and maximally
thick ink for the
second color.
B. Remix the ink
with less
transparent base.

C. Allow first color to
dry thoroughly
before printing
second.
D. None, if Solution
A does not work.
E. Use a single
squeegee stroke.

Preventions: A. See Solution A.
B. through E. Print
each color as
thinly as possible.

16. The edges of shapes along the
outside of the print do not print clearly
and build up a thick deposit of ink.

Causes: A. Printing too close
to the edge of
tape, paper mask
or block-out.
Squeegee is riding
up on mask,
preventing good
contact with the
printing paper.
B. Squeegee too wide.

Solutions: A. and B. Use a
squeegee long
enough to cover
the stencil image
but short enough to
avoid riding on tape
or paper masks.

Preventions: A. and B. Keep stencil
dimensions about
one to two inches
from paper or tape
masks. If possible,
use a liquid
block-out.

17. Black spots appear in light colors.

Causes: A. Black neoprene
squeegee blade.
B. Contaminated ink.
C. Dust particles from
squeegee
sharpening.

Solutions: A. Use a tan neoprene
or plastic
squeegee.
B. None.
C. Take several
proofs on scrap
paper. If spots
remain, scrub the
spotted screen
areas thoroughly
with solvent.

Preventions:	A.	See Solution A.
		B.	Clean containers and tools for mixing ink and screen.
		C.	Clean screen of dust before printing.

18.	Streaks of foreign color appear in a solid area.
	Causes:	A.	Dirty squeegee.
		B.	Dirty screen.
		C.	Ink not mixed thoroughly.
	Solutions:	A.	Clean squeegee thoroughly and print several proofs on scrap paper.
		B.	None.
		C.	Remove the ink and mix it until all streaking disappears.
	Preventions:	A. and B.	Always clean the screen and all tools thoroughly after printing.
		C.	See Solution C.

19.	Transparent streaks of color appear in solid areas.
	Cause:		Particles of unmixed transparent base.
	Solution:		Remove the ink and mix it thoroughly to remove lumps. Print several proofs on scrap paper until streaking stops.
	Prevention:		See Solution.

20.	Fine details (dots, fine lines, etc.) slowly disappear (plug up) during printing.
	Causes:	A.	Thick ink.
		B.	Insufficient transparent base.
		C.	Fast drying ink.
		D.	Dull squeegee.
		E.	Old multifilament fabric.
		F.	Delay between printings.
	Solutions:	A.	Remove the ink and thin it with appropriate thinner.
		B.	Remove the ink and add transparent base.
		C.	Remove the ink and add a retarder thinner or use a flood stroke between prints.
		D.	Clean and resharpen the squeegee.
		E. and F.	Employ a flood stroke.
	Preventions:	A. through C.	See Solutions A through C.
		D.	Use a squeegee with a plastic blade.
		E.	Use screens with fabric in good condition.
		F.	See Solution F.

21.	A ghost image (double image) appears on the prints.
	Causes:	A.	Use of multiple squeegee strokes.
		B.	Ink from print offsetting onto underside of screen.
		C.	Paper shifting after screen is lowered and before printing.
	Solutions:	A.	Print with single squeegee stroke. Print on scrap paper until ghost disappears.
		B. and C.	Make sure paper or screen does not shift while the two are in contact. Make several proofs on scrap paper until ghost disappears.
	Preventions:	A. through C.	See Solutions A through C.

22.	Although all stencils were cut in register to each other, a second stencil is now too small for a previously printed one.
	Causes:	A.	Change in size of paper after

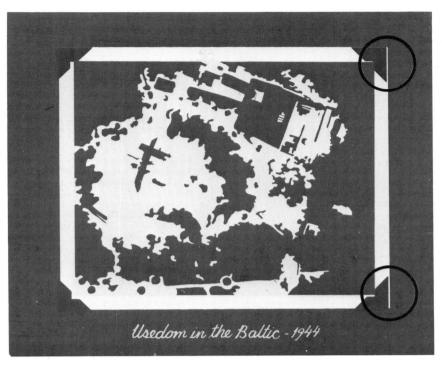

Usedom in the Baltic - 1944

8.22 Side misregister. Note white lines at right sides of triangular photo tabs.

printing, due to change in humidity.

B. Change in size of screen after stencil was adhered, due to change in humidity.

C. Change in a non-moistureproof stencil before adhesion due to change in humidity.

Solutions: None.

Preventions:
A. All printing paper should be brought into the printing area and allowed to adjust to humidity conditions before printing.

B. Avoid printing or adhering on exceedingly dry or humid days when using silk fabrics. In this respect, synthetics are better.

C. Use stencil materials that have a moistureproof or dimensionally stable backing sheet.

23. Left and right registration shift periodically in spite of care in registration. (Figure 8.22).

Causes:
A. Loose hinges on screen.

B. Variation in the way in which the screen is lowered before each print.

Solutions:
A. Tighten all screws. If pins are loose, bend them slightly.

B. Always raise and lower the screen in the same way, with the same hand. If play is unavoidable, push the screen to one side before each print.

Preventions:
A. Use tight hinges and replace them if they become very loose.

B. See Solution B.

24. Registration tabs are accurate and stencil is accurately registered, but every other print is off register at the top or bottom.

Causes: A. Slack screen.
               B. Change in direction of squeegee stroke every other print.

Solutions: A. and B. Print all prints in the same direction.

Preventions: A. Restretch the fabric or replace it.
               B. With large screens it is sometimes necessary to deliberately mis-register a stencil high on the screen to take into account the shift in the fabric when the squeegee is pulled toward you. Prints must be printed in the same direction.

25. Streaks appear in crayon texture areas of a resist stencil.

Cause: Beads or drops of glue were permitted to dry on the stencil.

Solution: Scrub gently with a brass suede brush.

Prevention: Apply glue thinly in a snowplow fashion, picking off any excess before it dries.

26. During printing of a glue-resist stencil, pinholes develop that are too extensive to paint out (Figure 8.23).

Causes: A. Glue mixed too thinly.
               B. Glue applied too thinly.
               C. Old or spoiled glue.
               D. Excessive scrubbing with a suede brush.

Solutions: A., B., and D. Stiffen the ink to decrease its ability to pass through the pin- holes. Or, after printing one impres- sion, wait a few moments to allow the ink in the pinholes to plug up.
               C. None. It will con- tinue to break down.

Preventions: A. Use fresh glue and mix with water in equal parts.
               B. Apply at least two coats of glue.
               C. If glue becomes exceedingly cloudy or foul-smelling, discard it.

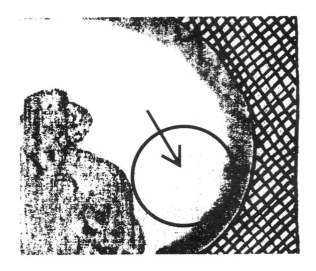

8.23 Comparison of an early (top) and later print, showing the development of pinholes.

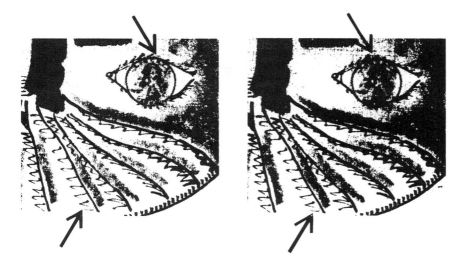

8.24   Comparison of an early (left) and later print, showing the plugging up of fine detail in a resist stencil.

D.   Use the suede brush only as needed and with as little pressure as possible.

27.   During printing of a resist stencil, fine textures are slowly plugging up and disappearing (Figure 8.24).

Causes:
A.   Stiff ink.
B.   Dull squeegee.
C.   Delay between prints.
D.   Rapid ink drying.

Solutions:
A.   Remove the ink and thin it.
B.   Sharpen the squeegee.
C.   Speed the printing or employ a flood stroke.
D.   Remove ink and remix with a retarder thinner, or use a flood stroke.

28.   During printing, fine textures bleed together into a solid area of color (Figure 8.25).

Causes:
A.   Thin or watery ink.
B.   Soft or dull squeegee.
C.   Multiple squeegee strokes.
D.   Too frequent use of flood stroke.

Solutions:
A.   Remove the ink and add transparent base to it. Print several impressions on scrap paper without ink until bleeding stops.
B.   Replace with sharper or harder squeegee, and print several impressions on scrap paper without ink until bleeding stops.
C.   Print as above and then continue, using only single squeegee strokes.
D.   Use a flood stroke only when necessary to clear clogged or plugged-up areas.

Preventions:
A.   through D.   Follow Solutions A through D.

8.25   Comparison of properly printed image and one in which fine detail has blurred together.

29. A hole slowly develops in the fabric during printing.

    Causes: A. A drop of glue or shellac on the printing surface.
                 B. Old silk.
    Solutions: A. Remove all bumps and lumps from the printing surface.
                 B. None.
    Preventions: A. Maintain a clean, smooth printing surface.
                 B. Replace the screen.

DECAL PRINTING

Decals are widely used on surfaces where it is difficult to print directly. The image is printed on a temporary support and transferred to the final surface at a later time. A familiar decal is the municipal sticker on the inside of an automobile windshield. Others include emblems and insignia on trucks and aircraft, store windows, and ceramics.

A requirement of decal inks is that they be tough and flexible. Those most frequently used are the decal lacquers and some types of enamels.

The most common decals use a temporary paper support that comes with a water-soluble layer on top. A coat of clear, heavy lacquer slightly larger than the image is printed onto the paper and then the colors of the image are screened on. A final coat of lacquer or varnish is printed on top. The lacquer or varnish layers increase the strength of the decal, making it less susceptible to damage when it is being transferred.

The sequence of printing the colors depends on how the decal will be transferred and on whether it will be viewed from the side that it is adhered to or through a clear material.

SIMPLEX DECALS

Simplex decals are generally used for interior applications and where the water-soluble coating is used as the adhesive in the final transfer.

The decal is soaked in warm water for a few moments and then placed face up on the desired surface. The paper backing sheet is slid out from beneath the decal. Air bubbles are removed by gentle rubbing from the center outward.

Large decals, which risk damage if slid off the paper, can be applied face down. In this case a coating of a decal adhesive must be printed on top of the final coat of clear lacquer. To transfer, the decal is soaked in water and then placed face down on the new surface. The backing sheet is peeled away, and the decal is squeegeed down to remove air bubbles. Excess adhesive from the paper backing is then washed off.

If the slide-off type of decal is to be viewed from the same side that it is applied to, the colors are printed face up, just as one normally prints on paper (Figure 8.26).

8.26 A decal printed face up. Six printings were required: glue, varnish, white, yellow, red, and a final coat of varnish. E—first printing, glue coat; C—second printing, first varnish coat; A—third printing, white background; B—fourth and fifth printings, yellow and red; D—last printing, last varnish coat. A face-down decal would be printed in the reverse order.

If the decal is to be viewed from the side opposite adhesion, as through glass, it is printed face down. It appears as a mirror image on the decal paper, and the color that is normally printed last is printed first.

With a decal that is applied face down and that is to be viewed from the same side as applied, it appears as a mirror image on the decal paper, and the colors are printed in a reverse sequence: the last color printed on paper is the first printed on the decal.

If the decal is to be viewed from the opposite side, then the image is printed face up as it would appear on paper, and the sequence of color printing is the same as when printing on paper.

DUPLEX DECALS

For durability in exterior applications, duplex decal paper, composed of two layers, with a water-soluble adhesive on top, is used. These decals are always applied face down.

To adhere them, a thin coat of clear lacquer or enamel is applied to the front of the decal. When it is tacky, the decal is placed face down on the final surface and squeegeed down tight, and the first layer of paper is removed. This layer can be sponged with water to facilitate its removal. The decal is squeegeed again, and when the lacquer or enamel is dry, water is used to remove the second layer of paper. The decal is then washed to remove any glue. Added durability is achieved by coating the decal with varnish.

DRY DECALS

Dry decals are adhered by a pressure-sensitive adhesive coating. Before printing the decal, this adhesive can be printed onto a special release paper, or the decal can be printed on simplex paper with a final coat of pressure-sensitive adhesive being applied on top of the decal.

With simplex paper, the decal is adhered face down, and the paper backing is removed with water. With release paper, it is applied face up.

When durability is not important, ordinary poster-type screen inks can be used in place of lacquers or enamels. Binding or overprint varnishes can be used for the first and last coats. It is recommended that transparent base be used minimally when preparing inks in order to prevent cracking or crazing of the printed image. If it is necessary to reduce inks for transparent effects, use a crystal clear or toner base instead of transparent base.

PRINTING ON PLASTIC

There has been a dramatic rise in the popular interest in silkscreen printing on plastics. Two situations make such printing ideal: (1) when you wish to illuminate your work from behind, and (2) when you wish to transform the plastic into a three-dimensional form after printing.

As has been noted, there is available a wide variety of inks that are suitable for printing on plastics. As a rule, an ink is selected for its compatibility with the plastic to be printed on, for its transparency or opacity, for its finish, and for its heat-formable properties.

Some general-purpose plastic inks work well on a variety of plastics. These are usually acrylic resin inks, and they require the specific solvents and thinners recommended by the manufacturer. Practically all require the use of lacquerproof stencils (photo or hand-cut water-soluble), but most can be printed with ordinary meshes (12xx or finer).

Because these inks are exceedingly tacky, they print best with monofilament fabrics with off-contact printing.

When durability is not important, and no attempt to form the plastic after printing is contemplated, ordinary poster-type silkscreen inks can be used. The adhesion of these inks to plastic is poor, so minimum quantities of transparent base should be used, and some crystal clear or toner base should be added. Off-contact printing should be used to aid in leveling out the inks and to prevent the image from lifting off the plastic when the screen is raised. Printing an overprint varnish should be avoided because these inks, if rewetted, may lift off the plastic.

The plastics most commonly printed on are acrylics, cellulose acetates, polystyrenes, and vinyls. Of these, the vinyls are the most difficult because they require good ink compatibility to prevent ink from cracking or flaking off. All of these plastics may be heat-formed. The acrylics are more expensive than the others (Figure 8.27).

The most common method of heat forming consists of heating the plastic until it becomes soft and rubbery, lowering it over a mold or form, and sucking the plastic onto the mold by removing all the air with a vacuum pump.

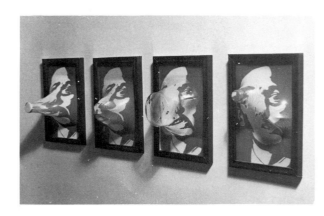

8.27   Plastic that has been printed and heat-formed.

Although vacuum-forming equipment is produced commercially, much of the equipment is custom-built. This equipment is not overly complicated, and a fairly simple vacuum-forming device can be built by anyone who wishes to work with plastics no bigger than 18″ x 24″.

For most work with thin, rigid plastics (.005 to .030 inch), an old vacuum cleaner motor and blower will produce a sufficient vacuum. A ballast tank is used to build up a vacuum. The pump evacuates the ballast tank, and the evacuated tank pulls the air from between the plastic and the mold.

The molds or forms can be objects placed on the table or molds built of wood or plaster. It is important that the molds you use not have undercut areas, or you will not be able to separate the plastic from the mold.

Most plastics soften readily between 200 and 300 degrees. Sufficient heat can be achieved by building a box lined with asbestos board and the element from a hotplate strung inside. This is suspended upside down over the sheet of plastic. When the plastic is sufficiently soft, usually indicated by drooping, it is lowered over the mold and the vacuum is turned on. The forming is instantaneous because the mold rapidly cools and hardens the plastic.

SILKSCREEN, ETCHING AND LITHOGRAPHY

It is possible to screen a heavy asphaltum varnish directly onto an etching or lithography plate (Figure 8.28), but because of the consistency of the asphaltum, fine detail may be lost.

There are several etching resists available that are intended for fine detail printing on metal plates. Many have the added advantage of drying rapidly. Some are modified vinyl types; others are modified asphaltum lacquers. Most require the use of lacquerproof stencils (photo, water-soluble). All can be printed with any type of screen fabric or mesh. All are completely resistant to the types and strengths of acid used in etching and lithography. And all are easily removed with lacquer thinners.

The principal application of etching resists comes in combining textural effects obtainable with silkscreen with the fine-line quality of etching or with the delicate shading of lithography.

With etching, since the nonprinting areas of the stencil will leave the metal exposed to the acid, a negative rather than a positive is used for the production of the photo stencil.

With lithography, a positive is used since the printed areas will remain ink-receptive.

GLASS ETCHING

Many suppliers carry materials that produce an etched surface when screened onto glass. These materials are water-soluble, requiring waterproof stencils. Any screen fabric may be used, but the mesh should not be finer than 14xx.

The material should be thoroughly mixed before printing. If it becomes crystallized, it should be placed in its container in a pan of hot water until the crystals disappear.

The glass should be thoroughly clean and free of grease. When printing, apply a flood stroke to ensure good passage of the etch. Allow the glass to sit a few minutes, then wash the etch off with cold water. Since the material rapidly sets in the screen, all printing should be completed before washing off the etch. The screen and all tools can be washed with cold water.

The glass etching is not deep (Figure 8.29). Repeated applications will enhance an etch to some degree, but it will never become dramatically deeper.

The effect of the etch is most dramatic when the glass is illuminated from the edge. The image then glows as if self-illuminated.

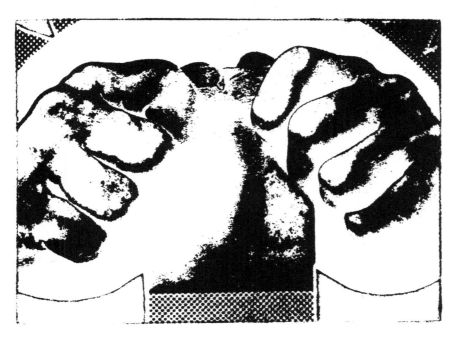

8.28 Etching made by printing asphaltum acid resist onto an etching plate. The same stencil was used in Figure 5.19

8.29 Glass etched by silkscreen.

BEADING AND FLOCKING

On occasions one may want a surface texture other than the appearance of the ink on the paper. One way to alter the surface is to use the ink as an adhesive for some other material. Two of the most common materials are extremely fine glass beads and colored rayon fibers (flocking). These materials are sprinkled onto the tacky ink and shaken around until uniformly distributed.

Although normal poster inks can be used to hold the flocking or beads, they do not have great binding power, and the materials tend to abrade off easily. Gloss enamels and various varnishes work well because they are inherently tacky.

Since the glass beads are colorless, the color is printed before applying the beads. Flocking is colored, so clear varnish can be used; color mixing can be achieved here by printing in one color and applying flocking of another color.

The glass beads are commonly used to reflectorize surfaces, such as highway signs, for improved viewing at night. The flocking is used wherever a velvetlike surface is desired, as in many greeting and novelty cards and some wall coverings.

Other fine, relatively uniform materials such as sand or sawdust can be used to achieve unusual surface textures.

TEXTILE PRINTING

It is beyond the scope of this book to go into fabric printing in any detail. Still, when printing an image, one occasionally has a strong urge to see how it will look on cloth or on an article of clothing.

Although ordinary silkscreen poster inks are not well suited for printing on fabrics, for novelty effects, where washability and colorfastness are not particularly important, these inks can be printed on cotton materials like T-shirts and sweat shirts with good results. The image will not run with repeated washings, but it will fade fairly rapidly.

These inks do not have to be altered in their properties for such printing. Except for a cardboard insert to keep the clothing flat during printing, no special equipment is necessary. Since most fabrics used are soft and absorbent, a thicker deposit of ink is usually required, so a soft or slightly dull squeegee should be used.

appendixes

INK APPLICATIONS CHART

		Acid Resist	Polyethylene	Fluorescent	General Plastic	Acetate	Acrylic	Mylar	Vinyl Gloss	Vinyl Flat	Thermoset	Epoxy	Enamels	Lacquers	Poster Process
		PRINTING INK													
TYPE	Evaporation	X	X	X	X	X	X	X	X	X				X	X
	Oxidation		X										X		
	Catalytic											X			
	Heat										X				
FINISH	Gloss		X		X	X	X	X	X		X	X	X	X	X
	Flat			X		X		X		X	X	X	X	X	X
FABRIC	Silk	X	X	X	X	X	X		X	X			X	X	X
	Nylon	X	X	X	X	X	X	X	X	X	X	X	X	X	X
	Dacron	X	X	X	X	X	X		X	X			X	X	X
	Polyester	X	X	X	X	X	X	X	X	X	X	X	X	X	X
	Stainless	X	X	X	X	X	X	X	X	X			X	X	X
STENCIL	Lacquer			X									X		X
	Indirect Photo	X	X	X	X	X	X	X	X	X	X	X	X	X	X
	Direct Photo	X	X	X	X	X	X	X	X	X	X	X	X	X	X
	Water-Soluble	X	X	X	X	X	X	X	X	X	X	X	X	X	X
MATERIAL	Paper			X									X	X	X
	Cardboard			X									X	X	X
	Masonite												X		X
	Metal	X									X	X	X	X	
	Glass										X	X	X	X	
	Foil							X			X		X	X	
	Leather													X	
	Ceramics											X			
	Wood												X	X	
	Cellulose Acetates				X	X	X		X				X	X	
	Polystyrene				X		X					some plastics			
	Acrylics				X		X								
	Rigid Vinyl				X		X	X	X						
	Flexible Vinyl						X	X	X	X					
	Polyethylene		X										X		
	Polyester							X							
	Textiles														
SCREEN MESH		12xx-20xx	230-45	8xx-14xx	12xx-16xx, 200-30	230-405	12xx-14xx	230-65	12xx, 230	10xx-14xx, 230	8xx-16xx	12xx-16xx	10xx-16xx, 200-305	12xx-16xx, 230	12xx-16xx, 160-230

MESH EQUIVALENCY CHART

SILK		DACRON		NYLON	POLYESTER
6xx	70–75	6xx	74–76	70–83	86
8xx	86	8xx	86	83–95	86–110
10xx	105–109	10xx	109–110	103–114	110–125
12xx	124–125	12xx	124–125	120–160	125–160
14xx	138–139	14xx	135–140	160–200	160–200
16xx	152–157	16xx	157	220–245	200–245
18xx	160–166	18xx	166	260–306	262–305
20xx	173–176	20xx	175	305–335	305–330
25xx	193–200	25xx	197	340–380	350–390

SOLVENT AND CHEMICAL USE CHART

	Acetone	Isopropyl Alcohol	Methyl Alcohol	Ethyl Alcohol	Ethylene Dichloride	Methyl Chloride	Mineral Spirits	Turpentine	Kerosene	Xylol	Butyl Cellosolve	White Vinegar	Water	Lacquer Thinner	Trisodium Phosphate	Hydrogen Peroxide	Enzyme	Naphtha	Benzene	Potassium Bichromate	Ammonium Bichromate	Chlorine Bleach
Process Ink Thinner							X		X	X												
Process Ink Clean-up							X	X		X								X	X			
Lacquer Ink Thinner														X								
Lacquer Ink Clean-up														X								
Enamel Thinner							X			X												
Enamel Clean-up							X	X		X												
Hide Glue Solvent													X									
Water-Soluble Block-out Remover		X	X	X	X								X									
Water-Soluble Block-out Thinner		X	X	X	X																	
Lacquer Stencil Adherer	X													X								
Lacquer Stencil Remover	X	X												X								
Water-Soluble Stencil Adherer		X										X	X									
Water-Soluble Stencil Remover												X	X									
Indirect Photo Stencil Developer																X						
Indirect Photo Stencil Wash-out													X									
Indirect Photo Stencil Remover													X				X					
Direct Photo Stencil Wash-out													X									
Direct Photo Stencil Remover	X																					X
Nylon Screen Prep													X									
Enzyme Neutralizer													X									
Fabric Degreaser													X		X							
Shellac Solvent		X	X																			
Screen Spot Remover	X			X																		
Photo Screen Sensitizer																				X	X	

glossary

ACETATE: A cellulosic plastic that can be silkscreened and heat-formed. Also used in preparing handmade positives for photo stencils.

ACETATE BUTYRATE: An extruded thermoplastic that can be silkscreened and heat-formed.

ACETIC ACID: Commonly used in a 5 percent solution (white vinegar) to prepare nylon screens for photographic stencils and to neutralize enzyme stencil removers.

ACETONE: An aromatic hydrocarbon ingredient in lacquer thinners and certain adhering fluids. Also used to remove stubborn spots of lacquer stencil and direct photo stencil emulsion.

ACID RESISTS: Commonly, asphaltum-type materials that can be silkscreened onto etching plates and serve as a block-out to subsequent etching of the plate.

ACRYLIC PAINTING MEDIUM: An acrylic polymer emulsion used in the preparation of lift transfers.

ACRYLIC PLASTIC: An optically clear cast resinous plastic that can be silkscreened and heat-formed.

ADHERE TO: The process of attaching a solvent-type knife-cut stencil or an indirect photo stencil to the screen.

ADHERING FLUID: The solvent used to adhere solvent-adhering knife-cut stencils.

ALCOHOL: Ethyl, methyl, and isopropyl alcohols are commonly used in silkscreen.

ALUMINUM STEARATE (Oxide): A principal thickening agent used in many silkscreen inks and transparent and extender bases.

AMMONIUM BICHROMATE: A light-sensitive chemical used to sensitize photo stencil materials.

ARC LAMP: A high-intensity light that operates by an electric current arcing between two carbon rods. Used commercially in exposing photo stencils.

BACKING SHEET: A thin, translucent or transparent paper or plastic that functions as a temporary support for knife-cut and indirect photo stencils until the stencil is adhered to the screen.

BASE: The side opposite the photosensitive emulsion of indirect photo stencils or photographic films.

BASEBOARD: The printing surface to which a portable screen is attached.

BEADING: Fine glass beads that are applied to varnish or inks while still wet to create reflectorized surfaces.

BI-LINE CUTTER: Stencil knife that cuts two parallel lines simultaneously.

BINDING VARNISH: A varnish used as an adhesive for beading, flocking, or laminating.

BLADE, SQUEEGEE: The rubber or rubber-like printing edge of the squeegee.

BLOCK-OUT: Methods or materials used to prevent unwanted areas of the screen from printing.

BLOT AND PRESS METHOD: Method of adhering solvent stencils when the backing sheet has become severely creased.

BLOTTING: Picking up excess water after adhesion of a photo stencil.

BURNISHER: A blunt, smooth-surfaced instrument used to apply rub-down and dry-transfer photomechanical materials.

CALENDER: A textured surface on paper created during its manufacture.

CARBON TISSUE: The original photo stencil technique in which a pigmented layer of gelatin on thin tissuelike paper is sensitized, exposed, and adhered to the screen.

CATALYTIC INKS: Inks that require the addition of a catalyst to bring about the chemical reaction necessary to effect a "cure."

CELLULOSE ACETATE: An extruded thermoplastic that can be silkscreened and heat-formed.

CHLORINE BLEACH: Common household bleach used full strength to remove direct-emulsion stencils.

CLEAN-UP: The procedure following printing for removing all traces of printing ink from the screen, squeegee, and other tools.

CONTACT FRAME: The system for creating tight, uniform contact between a positive and a photo stencil during exposure.

CONTACT PRINTING: Silkscreen printing in which the screen is in close contact with the material being printed.

CONTE CRAYON: A soft, chalklike drawing material that can be used in producing handmade positives.

DACRON: A synthetic fiber used to make multifilament screen fabrics.

DECALS (Decalcomania): Process of printing onto a temporary support that can be removed by soaking in water and the print transferred to another surface. Commonly used in ceramic decoration.

DEGREASE: To remove all grease, oil, or ink residue from the screen fabric.

DEVELOPER: Chemical(s) used to process photosensitive materials after exposure.

DIMENSIONAL STABILITY: The degree to which a material is not affected by changes in temperature and humidity.

DIRECT EMULSION: Polyvinyl alcohol/polyvinyl acetate solutions that are made light-sensitive and coated onto the screen prior to exposure in producing a photo stencil.

DIRECT METHOD: The process of making a direct-emulsion stencil.

DRYING RACK: An arrangement for keeping the prints separate while they dry.

DRYPOINT POSITIVE: Positive made by scratching lines into sheet plastic and then filling them in with opaque ink. Used in making photo stencils.

DRY-TRANSFER PHOTOMECHANICAL MATERIALS: A group of photomechanical aids that permit direct application of textures, patterns, symbols, and letters to another surface. Used in the preparation of handmade positives and with resist stencils.

DUROMETER: A hardness scale used in rating the hardness of squeegee blades.

EMULSION: The light-sensitive, light-hardening material used to make photo stencils, either PVA or gelatin.

ENAMELS: Inks that dry by oxidation, commonly used for exterior applications.

ENZYME: A gelatin solubilizer used to remove gelatin photo stencils.

ETHYL ALCOHOL: Commonly used to dilute shellac.

ETHYL CELLULOSE: A type of ink that dries by solvent evaporation. Most frequently used for printing on paper and interior applications. Commonly called process ink.

ETHYLENE DICHLORIDE: Solvent found in many types of commercial water-soluble fill-in solutions. Used to thin or remove stubborn spots from the screen.

EVAPORATION INKS: Inks that dry by solvent evaporation.

EXPOSURE: The procedure of shining the appropriate light through a positive so that it strikes the photosensitive material beneath.

EXPOSURE FRAME: See Contact Frame.

EXPOSURE UNIT: The light source or system used in exposing photo stencil materials.

EXTENDER: Materials added to inks to reduce opacity or increase coverage.

EYEBALLING: Judging registration or placement of prints during printing by visual inspection.

FABRIC: The finely woven, open material that is stretched on the frame to form the screen.

FILL-IN: See Block-out.

FILM: Generally refers to photographic materials used in cameras.

FILM POSITIVE: A positive that is made with photographic film.

FIXATIVE: A clear acrylic spray used to preserve handmade positives.

FLOCKING: Short rayon fibers of various colors. Used to create a velvetlike texture when applied to wet inks or varnish.

FLOOD METHOD: A method of adhering solvent stencils in which fairly large quantities of solvent are applied and mopped up rapidly.

FLOOD STROKE: The act of dragging ink across the screen with the squeegee without transferring the ink to the printing surface below. Used to free clogged or plugged printing areas.

FRAME: Usually refers to the rectangular structure across which the screen fabric is stretched.

FRISKET KNIFE: A thin-handled, small-bladed knife used for cutting stencils.

GELATIN: A water-soluble protein that can be made light-sensitive and light-hardening. Commonly used with indirect photo stencils.

GLASS ETCH: Any of several compounds that permit the frosting of glass by printing directly with silkscreen.

GLOSSY: A high-gloss black-and-white photograph.

GLUE: See Hide Glue.

GRAPHITE: A form of carbon used in pencils. In its softer forms it can be used in the preparation of handmade positives.

GUTTERS: The taped edges of the screen

parallel to the direction of the squeegee.

HANDMADE POSITIVE: A positive that is made by direct application of opaque materials to a transparent or translucent sheet of plastic.

HALFTONE: A film positive made from a photograph in which all the grays have been translated into dots of black and white.

HIDE GLUE: A glue made from animal hides and used as a block-out and in the preparation of resist stencils.

HINGE: Used to attach the screen in a fixed position to the printing surface; allows the screen to be swung out of the way to place paper beneath.

HINGE CLAMP: A special hinge that is attached permanently to the printing surface, which has provision for clamping of screen frames.

HOT INKS: Inks that are melted to the proper consistency by using an electrically heated screen, rather than being thinned to printing consistency.

HYDROGEN PEROXIDE: A chemical used as a hardener/developer in dilute form for many indirect photo stencils.

INDIA INK: A common drawing ink (black) used for the production of handmade positives of camera-ready art.

INDIRECT PHOTO STENCIL: Any photo stencil process in which the stencil is prepared, exposed, and developed prior to adhesion to the screen.

INK: Any of many materials used in silkscreen printing.

INK RESERVOIR: See Well.

ISOPHORONE: A solvent thinner for certain types of vinyl inks.

ISOPROPYL ALCOHOL: Used to chill, reduce swelling, and speed drying of photo stencils. Also an ingredient in adhering fluids for certain types of water-soluble knife-cut stencils.

KEROSENE: A thinner used with ethyl cellulose inks to increase the drying time.

KNIFE-CUT STENCIL: Any stencil material that is prepared by cutting and removing the areas that will print.

KRAFT GUMMED TAPE: A brown paper tape with a water-soluble glue adhesive. Used to mask screens and to make registration tabs.

LACQUER: Evaporation paints or inks used in printing of decals and for blocking out unwanted portions of the screen.

LACQUER STENCIL: A knife-cut stencil made of a lacquerlike material laminated to a thicker temporary support.

LACQUER THINNER: A family of solvents; they are used with lacquer inks, paints, and stencils.

LATEX: Principal ingredient in liquid maskoids or liquid friskets. Used in the preparation of resist stencils.

LIFT TRANSFER: A technique for making positives in which an image printed on clay-coated paper is separated from the paper and transferred to a transparent or translucent plastic sheet.

LIGHT-HARDENING: A property of photo stencil emulsions. Prior to exposure these emulsions are water-soluble; after exposure they are not.

LIGHT TABLE: A table with a translucent glass (plastic) top with lights below. Used to aid in the preparation of positives and in exposing photo stencils.

LINE POSITIVE: A photographic positive in which all the grays have been translated into either opaque black or clear white.

LIQUID FRISKET: A water-soluble latex solution that becomes water-insoluble when dry. Used in the preparation of resist stencils.

LITHO CRAYON: A black wax crayon available in several hardnesses in either stick or pencil form. Used in preparing resist stencils and handmade positives.

MASK: The taped portion of the screen.

MASKOID: See Liquid Frisket.

MATTE ACETATE: Acetate plastic that has a frosted surface.

MESH: Refers to the number of threads per inch in screen fabrics.

MESH COUNT: See Mesh.

METHYL ALCOHOL: Used in combination with ethylene dichloride as a solvent and thinner for some types of water-soluble block-outs. Can also be used to remove lacquer knife-cut stencils from the screen.

METHYL CHLORIDE: Used in combination with ethyl alcohol as a solvent and thinner with some types of water-soluble block-outs.

MINERAL SPIRITS: A solvent commonly used with ethyl cellulose process or poster inks.

MONOFILAMENT FIBER: Threads (of a screen fabric) that are composed of a single continuous fiber.

MULTIFILAMENT FIBER: Threads that are composed of many very fine, (discontinuous) fibers.

NEGATIVE: A film image in which all lights and darks are reversed from the original scene, artwork, or photograph.

NITROCELLULOSE: The base for many lacquer inks.

NYLON: A monofilament fiber fabric frequently used when printing with photo stencils.

OPAQUE: A condition in which no light is permitted to pass through.

OVERLAP: The degree to which stencil shapes are made larger than desired to ensure that subsequently printed colors will appear in register.

OVERPRINT VARNISH: A varnish that is printed over the print, either to achieve a glossy surface or for protection.

OXIDATION INKS: Inks that undergo a chemical change upon exposure to air, becoming insoluble in their original solvent when dry.

PACK-UP: A built-up surface beneath the screen, used to ensure good contact between the stencil and the screen during adhesion.

PEROXIDE: See Hydrogen Peroxide.

PHOTO OPAQUE: A liquid material used to block out unwanted portions of film positives or negatives and in producing handmade positives.

PLATING RESISTS: Materials that can be silkscreened onto nonconductive substrates and that are unaffected by electrolytic solutions.

POLYESTER: A monofilament fabric used when good dimensional stability and durability are needed.

POLYSTYRENE: A thermoplastic that can be silkscreened and heat-formed.

POLYVINYL ACETATE: A principal ingredient in direct-emulsion coatings.

POLYVINYL ALCOHOL: A common ingredient in direct-emulsion coatings. Also used as a release agent in plastic casting.

POTASSIUM BICHROMATE: A light-sensitive chemical used to sensitize photo stencil materials.

PREP: The materials and process of preparing a screen for receiving photographic stencils.

PRESENSITIZED FILM: A photo stencil material that is light-sensitive as purchased.

PRESSMANSHIP: The ability to make each print identical and to solve quickly and effectively any problems that emerge during printing.

PRINT: The final form of the silkscreened image.

PUDDLE METHOD: A method of developing stencils without complete immersion in the developer.

PVA: An abbreviation for polyvinyl acetate/alcohol solutions used in direct emulsion stencils.

REGISTRATION: Printing images precisely where intended.

REGISTRATION TABS: Stops used to permit accurate placement of the printing material to achieve good registration.

RESIST: See Resist Stencils, Acid Resists, and Plating Resists.

RESIST STENCILS: Stencils prepared directly on the screen. The drawing materials and the stencil materials have different solvents and are resistant to one another.

SCREEN, TO: To translate the grays of a photograph into dots of black and white.

SCREEN: Generally refers to the frame with the fabric stretched across it.

SCREEN CARRIAGE: A system for hinging the screen to the printing surface, permitting accurate adjustment of the screen position.

SCREEN RECLAIMING: The procedure for removing a stencil from a screen and making it ready to accept a new stencil.

SCREEN STOP: Small blocks attached to the printing surface beside the screen to prevent the screen from shifting sideways.

SCREEN SUPPORT: System that keeps the screen in a slightly elevated position between printings.

SHOOTING: To expose photographic film or photo stencil materials.

SILKSCREEN PROCESSOR: A person or firm that makes screens with stencils for a silkscreen printer.

SIZING: A starchlike material in new silk that gives it body.

SOLUBILIZE: To render something soluble.

SOLUTION: A mixture of two or more compatible chemicals usually in liquid form.

SOLVENT: A substance, usually liquid, that dissolves another substance.

SQUEEGEE: The tool used to force the ink through the screen onto the printing material.

SQUEEGEE CARRIAGE: A system that holds the squeegee at the proper angle for printing. This is especially useful with very large screens.

STENCIL: That material on the screen that controls what will or will not print, thus creating the design on the printing material.

STENCIL KNIFE: Small-bladed knife with a handle about the size of a pencil, used to cut stencils.

STRETCHING THE SCREEN: The act of fastening the screen fabric to the screen frame under extreme tension.

STROKE: A single pass with the squeegee across the screen.

THERMOSETTING INKS: Inks that require the application of heat in order to reach their final "dry" state.

TRANSPARENT BASE: A gelatinous material composed of aluminum stearate (oxide) and mineral spirits and used to extend inks, make them more transparent, and give them body.

TRISODIUM PHOSPHATE: A degreasing agent used in prepping screens, formerly a common ingredient in household detergents.

TURPENTINE: A solvent used to clean up screens after printing, particularly ethyl cellulose inks.

ULTRAVIOLET LIGHT: The end of the spectrum beyond the visible portion of violet. Most photo stencil materials are particularly sensitive to ultraviolet light.

VEHICLE: A varnish or oil in which paints or ink pigments are suspended.

VINYL: A family of plastics that can be silkscreened and heat-formed.

WASH-OUT: The process of removing the unexposed portions of a photo stencil.

WASH-UP: The process of removing all ink from the screen after printing.

WATER-SOLUBLE BLOCK-OUT: Any liquid block-out material that is impervious to ink and easily removed with water.

WELL: The areas between the inside of the frame and the stencil at the front and back (head and tail) of the screen.

WHITE VINEGAR: A commonly available form of 5 percent acetic acid.

XYLOL: A thinner used when one wishes to accelerate the drying of ethyl cellulose inks. Can be used as a solvent for wash-up.

ZYLOL: An uncommon spelling of Xylol.

index